THE GREAT WESTERN
in the
WEST MIDLANDS

P. B. Whitehouse

Oxford Publishing Co.

BIBLIOGRAPHY

I have consulted the following works to obtain information used in this book and am most grateful to their compilers, authors and publishers for the dedication put in to them.

History of the Great Western Railway - *GWR and Ian Allan Ltd*
Locomotives of the Great Western Railway (12 books) - *Railway Correspondence and Travel Society*
Railways of the West Midlands, A Chronology, 1808-1954 - *Stephenson Locomotive Society*
Great Western Railways and Bradshaw's Timetables
Great Western Railway Engine Books
Railway Magazine

Notes and Acknowledgements

No well illustrated book, which covers a period of almost one hundred years, can come from one person's experiences, camera or knowledge. I am, therefore, very much indebted to the many who have helped me to gather material together for this volume. The majority of these contributors I am able to name but, sadly, a number of pictures and negatives, which have come into my collection, have no information regarding the name of the photographer concerned. To those who I am unable to acknowledge I should like to express my grateful thanks for this unknown help. If, however, anyone recognizes an unacknowledged photograph I should be delighted to hear from them, via the publisher.

This book is not a railway history, but I have tried to be as specific as possible with dates, although some have had to be approximate. Memories are not always exact and those photographs of boyhood days were taken in enthusiasm rather than for possible publication forty years ahead. Even with some of my own photographs I am not always sure as to the exact year in which they were taken. Where there is doubt, this has been indicated in the caption. Of course, the first seventy years of the period can only be covered by illustrations from those no longer with us, and come partly from the Illustrated London News, which contains some superb Victorian railway material. Others come from Public Libraries and a few from private collections and the National Railway Museum. These I acknowledge with thanks. Irene Kent has been more than helpful in ensuring that I was able to find photographs from the City of Birmingham Public Library. Local

friends and photographers have also been very kind. C. C. Green and John Burman have allowed me to use some of those fascinating photographs which were taken by H. W. Burman in the Edwardian era, Derek Harrison has sifted through his spare Snow Hill pictures and Roger Carpenter has done the same over a broader area. Of my photographer friends, I can only say that without their help there would have been no book, of this nature, possible. Arthur Camwell has searched through his immense collection for pictures, Philip Hopkins, whose boyhood camera clicked so well in the 1920s and 1930s has a unique record, and Arthur Flowers has taken me through his magnificent collection. Of the remainder, most of the photographs come from my own collection; some like those of P. M. Alexander through the purchase of a collection and copyright, and others entering my collection over the years. Of the latter, I would particularly like to mention the late W. Leslie Good whose negatives, if only a few, I was able to rescue after his death. He was one of the best and perhaps most prolific of the Birmingham photographers of the 1920s and 1930s, and those of us who collected his photographs when we were younger have an excellent record of the railway working of that area around that time. Many of the photographs illustrated here, which have been credited to my collection are, quite possibly, from his camera.

Lastly, I should like to thank my wife and Christine Brook who have miraculously read my writing and have typed the introduction and captions; not an easy job but one well done.

P. B. Whitehouse
Birmingham
1983

Typesetting by:
Aquarius Typesetting Services, New Milton.

Printed in Great Britain by:
Balding + Mansell Ltd, Wisbech, Cambs.

Published by:
Oxford Publishing Co.
Link House
West Street
POOLE, Dorset

Contents

Chapter 1   Introduction

This book purports to be no more than an interesting, and often fascinating, record of things that happened on the Great Western Railway in the West Midlands. The boundaries are arbitrary as they tend to fit the pictures rather than particularly-designated areas. The subjects are mostly steam trains, generally on the stretches of line that I knew best and where I have wandered over the years as an enthusiast, and on my journeys to and from school. Historically, it has been possible to cover a period of almost one hundred years although the first fifty years have been condensed, through lack of material. In addition, I wanted to illustrate the familiar Great Western scene; the period of forty years, from the time of Edwardian redevelopment, to the end, in 1947.

My first recollections of the Great Western Railway were in the mid-1920s when, as a small boy, I was taken to Snow Hill Station, Birmingham on winter Saturday afternoons when my mother found it too cold standing by the touchline watching my father play hockey. Snow Hill, at that time, seemed to me to be vast and noisy. Unlike New Street where LMS trains rolled into the station, the Great Western ones roared into Snow Hill from a smoking tunnel and did not stop until halfway along No. 5 platform. The crowds, too, seemed greater, with large numbers coming out of the waiting and refreshment rooms as soon as they heard the familiar clang in the tunnel. Equally large crowds descended from the coaches and made their way past us and up the wide staircase to the circulating area and miniscule, though then adequate, car-park. To someone only just weaned on trains, and mostly LNWR ones to boot, these big engines with outside cylinders seemed a little frightening. This was made more so by the sharp Swindon bark as a London-bound express left for the Stygian gloom of the tunnel. Other platform memories, which I particularly remember, include the arrival of the through Kent and Sussex coast to Birkenhead train with its

green coaches and restaurant car. This was of great appeal as its arrival meant the trundling, from a corner of the station, of a kind of water cart with a big wheel on its side and a hosepipe, which was connected up to the restaurant car, the wheel being turned by a red-faced porter. It was all a little strange as no one thought to tell me that restaurant cars needed fresh water. Then, of course, there was the bookstall, Wyman's which dispensed copies of the Railway Magazine at one shilling (5p), Great Western jigsaw puzzles of 150 pieces at two shillings and six pence (12½p), books on Great Western matters, such as the 'Cornish Riviera Express' at one shilling and lead paperweights of engines which were termed an extravagance. For that matter, the other items mentioned were similarly termed, except on some special occasion. However, it was always a magnificent half-day as we could come into Birmingham and return on a rattling, sometimes solid-tyred, open top Corporation bus.

It took a further five years before Snow Hill and its environs came firmly into their own as, on holiday, I had made friends with a Stourbridge boy. Birmingham and Stourbridge were connected by the Great Western Railway. From then on, therefore, school holidays were spent taking engine names and numbers at both places. This was from 1932 onwards and, at the beginning of that period, the 4-4-0 'Bulldogs' were still working what was known as the Birmingham and South Wales Express where Stourbridge Junction was the second stop, the first being at Smethwick Junction, a relic of past days. In fact, it was not much of an express, as it also stopped at Kidderminster, Worcester and stations to Hereford and Cardiff; but it was just the train for me. From Stourbridge Junction, over the single line to Stourbridge Town, a service was run by a vertical-boilered steam railcar, the engine of which appeared to be hidden in the luggage compartment.

Fortunately, before too long, we discovered the secrets of this engine by talking to the drivers who actually gave us a ride; it was very hot. Stourbridge Junction, also, was a good place to watch trains, from the saddle tanks shunting the yard to 'Saints', 'Bulldogs' and the inevitable 2-6-2 tanks. However, the majority of the interest was at Snow Hill which was seldom quiet and even at the quiet periods there were still fascinating things to be investigated. There were slot machines where you could punch out your name on a piece of aluminium strip and a model of a GWR 'King' whose wheels went round, if someone could be persuaded to insert a penny. There were poster boards of far off places, often containing pictures of trains, and those dreadful crane machines with treasures dug deep into the piles of cylindrical sugar sweets, which were all that were retrieved in the feeble electric grab. There were cavernous subways with their glazed brick walls, huge toilets and the rarely-visited refreshment rooms presided over by ladies in black. Eating money, usually a penny, was not to be wasted and much thought was spent on whether to buy a bar of Nestle's or Fry's chocolate cream or a packet of Sun Raised Maidens. For the more adult, there were two Churchman's cigarettes available from the same machine.

The best place for watching trains was at the far end of the main 'down' platform as this afforded a full view of almost any movement, including a sight of anything sitting on one of the turntable roads, in the far distance, to the right of the Hockley Tunnel. The only real danger of missing anything was a slow departure of one of the heavy iron-ore trains, often behind the newly-converted 72XX 2-8-2 tanks, and this could block the view of most 'up' movements for a few minutes. By 1935/6, the modern classes were predominant; the 'Counties' had gone in 1934 and 'Bulldogs' were becoming more rare, although locomotives like *Pershore Plum* and *Peacock* arrived with monotonous regularity. Most of the locals were in the hands of 3150 and 51XX class 2-6-2 tanks and the Dudley autos were pushed and pulled by Class 64XX panniers. Stratford and West of England trains were hauled by 'Saints', which later worked some locals and the London trains were nearly always worked by 'Kings' except when the odd 'Castle' appeared, including the bullet-nosed No. 5005 *Manorbier Castle*. Sometimes we saw No. 2916 *Saint Benedict* with its eight-wheeled ex-*Great Bear* tender. At the end of the afternoon we would go to No. 7/12, the 'up' platform, and, sizzling there, making the odd rude noise, would be a 'King' on the 3.55p.m. to London. Across the platform's face would be a 'Star' on the 4.05p.m. semi-fast, which followed it, stopping at Hatton, Warwick, Leamington Spa, Banbury, Oxford and Reading, or so the train indicator board told us. Regular engines for this train were No. 4016 *Knight of the Golden Fleece* and No. 4018 *Knight of the Grand Cross*.

Trips by train were infrequent as these cost more than the penny in the platform ticket machine and pocket money was tight. However, occasionally, there was a foray, including a summer holiday trip to Banbury. This was an eagerly-anticipated event as it not only entailed a ride in a real express, but it also provided an opportunity to see something never seen in Birmingham; an LNER engine. Sadly there was not much variety as only three classes, to my memory, materialized, but all were ex-Great Central engines including those beautiful Atlantics.

Another chance of a Great Western journey would occur if I went to stay with my grandparents who lived in the little Worcestershire village of Cropthorne, whose nearest station was Fladbury, between Evesham and Pershore on the Oxford, Worcester & Wolverhampton line. The treat, however, was to come home, on my own, by train and there were actually four ways of doing this. These were by way of Worcester, then by the GWR, via Stourbridge, or by LMS via the Lickey; or by way of Evesham and Stratford-upon-Avon by the GWR or via Evesham, Redditch and Barnt Green to New Street on the LMS. I suppose that it would also have been possible to go on a Kingham-bound train and change at Honeybourne, but I do not remember knowing of this at the time. What I do remember is that on the first occasion on which I made this journey the train ended up at a place which I never knew existed; Birmingham Moor Street. However, my most regular travelling by Great Western was on the school train to Warwick during 1937 and 1938. For six days a week, during term time, I travelled on the 8a.m. 'all stations' to Leamington Spa from Snow Hill behind a 51XX class 2-6-2 tank and back from Warwick, on most days, on the 4.42p.m. which was nearly always hauled by a 'Saint'; often by No. 2902 *Lady of the Lake*. The only chance of getting a fast train was on the infrequent occasion of Warwick Races when we had card playing men, with breath smelling of beer, as companions, but this train was usually hauled by a 'Star' as compensation.

As one grew older, one also grew bolder and, in this case, boldness involved asking an engine crew of the early evening Snow Hill pilot, as it happened No. 2902, if I could go on the footplate and, later, have a ride. The pair concerned were both Leamington men; Albert Daniels and Walter Skelsey. I was very fortunate in gaining their friendship for, not only did they teach me a lot, they also gave me my first real Great Western footplate trips. They were absolute opposites, Albert Daniels was into his sixties, a teatotaller and a serious church-goer and Walter Skelsey was a cheerful wiry Welshman who liked his pint. Both were good Great Western men. I was always asked to show my ticket before I was allowed on the footplate and it was always in the dark so that a sixteen year old was not obvious. The most enjoyable trips were back from Stourbridge Junction as there was the climb up Cradley Bank to Old Hill and I sometimes wielded a shovel under Walter's eagle eye, usually on the, then new, 2-6-2 tank No. 8100.

Then came the war and a veil over railway enthusiasm as the King demanded my time. There were some out of the way trips like the ones at weekends from Bourton-on-the-Water to Cheltenham behind 'Dukedog' 4-4-0s, and the return on an Oxford train which was hauled by a blacked-out 'Castle'. The most welcome trip of all was the trip back from Hereford to Snow Hill behind a 'Star', at the end of a battle training course! During overseas service, I actually saw a real 'Dean Goods' in Algiers and more at Bari in Italy; the latter when we were flying Dakotas out to Tito's partisans; a marvellous combination. It was on demob leave when I came back to the Great Western. Sadly, not for long, but what there was was good - for it was then that my old friend Pat Garland introduced me to Bill Gillett and Maurice Long.

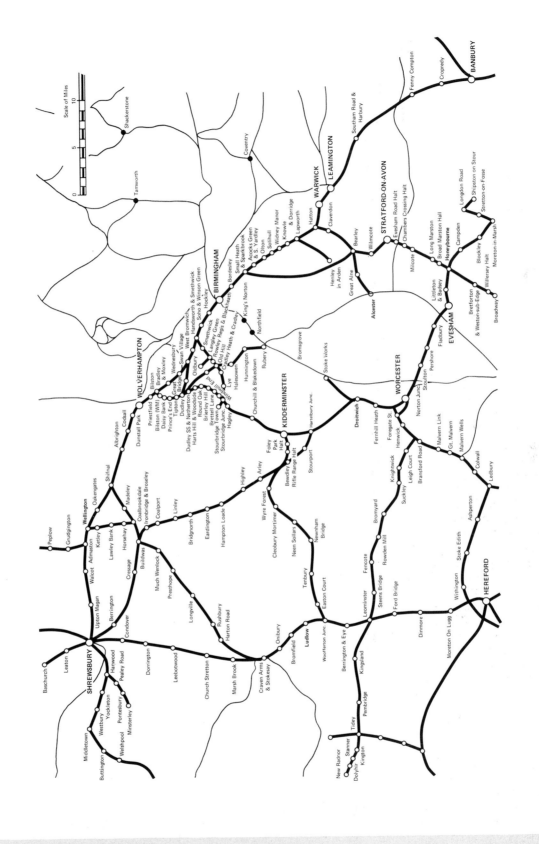

ENLARGED MAP OF BIRMINGHAM and DISTRICT

Scale of Miles

In 1946, when Bill was acting as relief signalman, he would take me round the various boxes in the Leamington/Stratford area and teach me the rudiments of block working. The real highlight, however, was the friendship with Maurice Long in Lapworth box. At that time, the Olton to Lapworth widening was twelve years old and, it seemed, only just adequate for the huge volume of traffic which flowed to and from Birmingham. The station was the last on the quadrupled track and the signal box, becaused of its position, was particularly busy. To the north was Knowle and Dorridge and to the south-east, was Rowington Junction. Maurice had the sections taped. He worked three shifts; 6 till 2, 2 till 10 and 10 till 6, and all were busy. If I ever want a mental picture of the Great Western, I think of those two years and that spot; the cheerful balding Maurice, in his uniform trousers and waistcoat, with his sleeves rolled up, flicking over those sometimes heavy levers, as if they were models, with duster in hand. The place was spotless, the lino polished, a newspaper was on the floor, the lever handles were bright steel and glistening. Any visiting fireman had to knock on the door and stand in the porch unless invited in. The weekends and evenings, spent in Lapworth box, were precious and very memorable; the ringing of the bells, the lights coming up on the track diagram above the levers, as the 'down' fast approached from Rowington, the 'King' class locomotive's tender dripping with water from the troughs, the roar of the engine as it passed and then the silence, bar the three rings pause one of 'train out of section'. Local trains came in and out with a few terminating; the smell of the railway was really there. Levers 73, 75, 76 and 78 controlled the starter, home, outer home and distant on the 'down' main and the latter two were a long distance away with the slack in the wires to be taken up causing those unknowing to get knocked flat on the floor. Maurice treated this as his best joke on the unwary

Plate 1: 'Saint' class 4-6-0, No. 2936 *Cefntilla Court,* takes water at Rowington Troughs, as it hauls a through Hastings to Birkenhead express, of Southern Railway stock, during the 1920s.

P. B. Whitehouse Collection

Plate 2: The Stourbridge Junction to Stourbridge Town (passenger station) branch used separate, but parallel, metals to the now closed line running down to the goods yard in the town. Opened in 1901, the motive power used varied from small tanks, on push-pull services, to railcars, either steam or diesel. The steam railcars' days were coming to an end in 1933 and this scene, of a unit approaching the Junction Station, was soon to disappear in favour of a 48XX 0-4-2T and trailer(s).

P. B. Whitehouse

Plate 3: Curved frame 'Bulldog' class 4-4-0, No. 3314 *Mersey,* is pictured at Stourbridge Junction in 1933, with a Birmingham to Worcester fast train. The station has two island platforms with the inner faces in general use for through services. At that period it was common practice to use both 'Bulldogs', and the remaining 'Counties' on the Birmingham-Worcester-Hereford trains.

P. B. Whitehouse

Plate 4: A trip freight from Bordesley Junction sidings to Hockley waits on the centre road at Snow Hill behind a new 0-6-0 pannier tank, No. 9759.

P. B. Whitehouse

Plate 5: The Leamington and Tyseley 'Saints' were often found on the 'all stations' Birmingham Division locals during the late 1930s. One of the regular performers was No. 2916 *Saint Benedict* which trailed the bogie tender from *The Great Bear*. The engine, is pictured at Widney Manor, at the head of one of the earlier wooden-bodied snap-handled suburban sets. If the window jammed in the up position it was impossible to get out! The train is the 5p.m. from Snow Hill to Leamington and the date is 1935.

P. Hopkins

Plate 6: Banbury Station, looking south, in the 1930s. The ex-Great Central Railway Atlantic, No. 5261 has just come off the shed which is situated beyond the picture on the 'down' side of the railway. It will shortly stand in the bay platform and wait to pick up a northbound fast train to Leicester and the Great Central main line.

P. B. Whitehouse Collection

Plate 7: One of the few Worcester Division 'Aberdare' class 2-6-0s, No. 2679, takes a freight past the old GWR shed at Gloucester, in 1937.

P. B. Whitehouse

Plate 8: A Leamington Spa to Birmingham (Snow Hill) and Wolverhampton (Low Level) 'all stations' train is about to pass over Rowington Troughs behind 51XX class, 2-6-2 tank, No. 5184. The train will have to run the full length of the platform at Snow Hill to enable the locomotive to take on water for the second stage of the journey.

P. B. Whitehouse Collection

Plate 9: Shrewsbury (Abbey) Station on a Sunday in August 1946. This was the terminus of the one time Shropshire & Montgomeryshire Railway which was taken over by the military during World War II. The train was an afternoon leave special, from the nearby Army camp at Nesscliffe. Unfortunately, the number of the engine, a 'Dean Goods' 0-6-0, was not taken but the coaches were ex-London, Tilbury & Southend Railway stock.

P. B. Whitehouse

Plate 10: Worcester Shed, in 1947, showing 0-4-2 tank, No. 3574, which was built in 1895.

P. B. Whitehouse Collection

Chapter 2   1852 to 1900

Plates 11, 12 & 13: The Oxford and Birmingham Railway was opened throughout on 30th September 1852, the contractor being Peto and Betts, working under the superintendence of I. K. Brunel. The opening was reported by *The Illustrated London News* on 16th October when it was given a full page including the three illustrations reproduced here. The whole of the work from Leamington and Warwick was constructed in 40 weeks. The text mentions Haycocks Green cutting and embankment, although the station and district (the village) were known as Acocks Green.

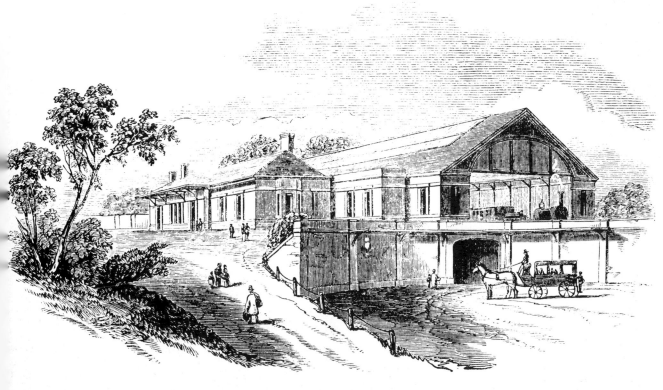

THE LEAMINGTON STATION

Plate 13

CUTTING AT HARBURY

Plate 14: Knowle Station, in 1891. Situated adjacent to the village of Dorridge, this station was not renamed Knowle & Dorridge until 1899. By now, the mixed gauge track, shown in the photograph of Solihull twenty seven years earlier, had been completely removed. At this period, the goods loops, to the north of the station, had not yet been installed. Later, the farm access bridge, whose outside arches took the loop lines, was demolished.

Green-Jacques

Plate 15: Wednesbury Station, in 1890. All trains between Birmingham and Wolverhampton were narrow gauge only after November 1868. The posed local train is behind, what appears to be, a 157 class 2-2-2 and consists of four clerestory vehicles with eliptical-roofed vans, with gas lighting. The signal arms do not seem to have spectacle plates attached. Enamelled advertisements include Fry's Cocoa, Sunlight Soap and Stevens Ink.

West Bromwich Reference Library, Metropolitan Borough of Sandwell

Plate 16: Olton Station, on 23rd March 1887, with Queen Victoria's Royal Train passing through. The occasion was the Queen's visit to Birmingham to lay the foundation stone of the Victoria Law Courts in Corporation Street.

City of Birmingham Reference Library

Plate 17: Solihull Station, clearly showing the dual gauge track. This rare photograph was taken in 1864.

City of Birmingham Reference Library

Plate 18: The remains of the incomplete viaduct which was originally intended to join the Birmingham & Oxford Junction Railway with the LNWR.

P. B. Whitehouse Collection

Plate 19: Snow Hill Station, looking north, in 1911.
D. Harrison Collection

**BIRMINGHAM
and DISTRICT
from 1908**

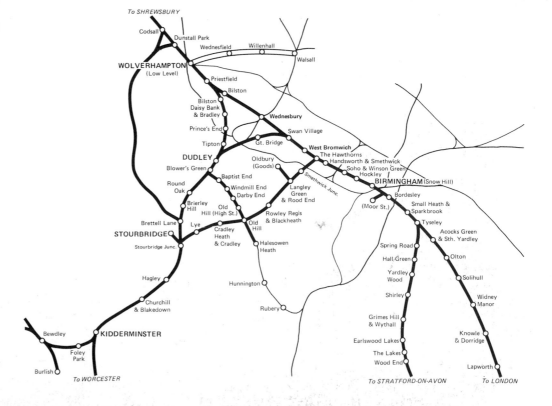

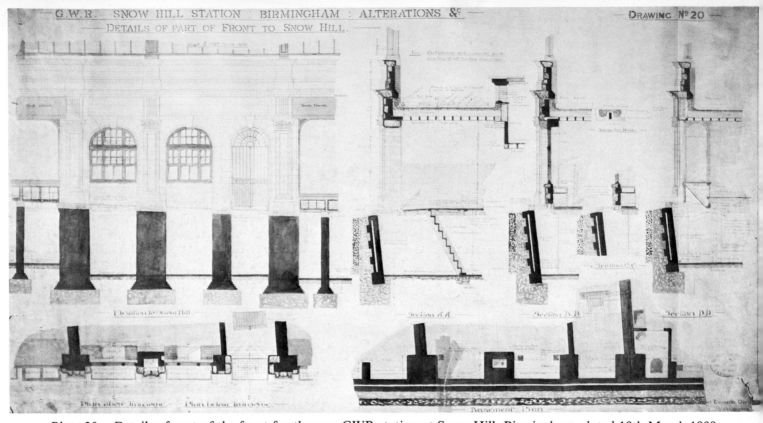

Plate 20: Details of part of the front for the new GWR station at Snow Hill, Birmingham, dated 10th March 1909. The design was by W. Y. Armstrong of the GWR and the contractor was Henry Lovatt Limited.

City of Birmingham Reference Library

Plate 21: Leamington Station, on 15th April 1911, with a northbound express, of clerestory stock, entering the station behind 'Atbara' class 4-4-0, No. 3394, carrying no nameplates. This was the earlier numbering, which was later changed to 4140. Its nameplate, *Adelaide*, had been removed five months earlier, in November 1910, to avoid confusion with the new 'Star' class 4-6-0, *Queen Adelaide*.

H. W. Burman/C. C. Green

Plate 22: Still with its tall chimney and dome, but now with top feed, 'Achilles' class 4-2-2, No. 3050 *Royal Sovereign* heads a 'down' local near Bentley Heath, around 1913/4.

H. W. Burman/C. C. Green

Plate 23: This photograph, taken on 3rd July 1911, at the north end of Knowle & Dorridge Station, shows 'Saint' class 4-6-0, No. 2909 *Lady of Provence,* with the 11.15a.m. 'up' express from Snow Hill. This is a sign of the times, as, in the previous September, the train was 4-4-0 hauled.

H. W. Burman/C. C. Green

Plate 24: Saddle tank 0-6-0, No. 1136, with a 'down' pick-up freight, is seen at Bentley Heath on September 1913. Driver Clifford is in the group of three. This 1874-built engine was not withdrawn until 1935 and it was fitted with pannier tanks in 1925.
H. W. Burman/C. C. Green

Plate 25: The 388 class or 'Armstrong Goods' 0-6-0 engines were the first of the GWR standard goods locomotives. Built between 1866 and 1876, they carried a variety of numbers and were in use all over the GWR system, some serving in far away lands during World War I. No. 716 is pictured at Knowle & Dorridge, around 1911.
H. W. Burman/C. C. Green

Plate 26: 'Flower' class 4-4-0, No. 4110 *Petunia,* with the 11.15a.m. ex-Snow Hill train, passing Bentley Heath, on 24th September 1910.
H. W. Burman/C. C. Green

Plate 27: The 'Cobham' class of 2-2-2s were built in 1879 for the narrow gauge expresses and were, in those early days, regular performers on the London to Birmingham (via Oxford) expresses. All but one of these locomotives were withdrawn by 1906. There is no doubt that the rapid influx of the more modern and powerful 4-4-0s, plus Churchward's 4-6-0s, put the final seal of doom on these engines. However, No. 165 remained in service for a further eight years, until 1914. It was fitted with ATC in 1906 and, during those last years, it was shedded at Oxford. It is pictured at Knowle & Dorridge, around 1913, with an 'up' local train.

H. W. Burman/C. C. Green

Plate 28: In 1913, a number of the Birmingham to London trains were still in the hands of the 4-4-0 locomotives. The 10.36 'up' train stands at Knowle & Dorridge, on 25th March, behind renumbered 'City' class, No. 3711 formerly 3434 *City of Birmingham*. The nameplate is in Birmingham's Museum of Science & Industry as part of the Cattell Collection. The 4-2-2 locomotives had, by this time, been generally displaced to local services.

H. W. Burman/C. C. Green

Plate 29: No. 3070 *Earl of Warwick,* another 'Achilles' class 4-2-2 locomotive, is seen with the 10.36a.m. 'up' train at Knowle & Dorridge on 29th August 1911. This was the first of the class to be fitted, in 1910, with a Belpaire boiler. Note that both the large dome and the tall thin copper-capped chimney were retained.

H. W. Burman/C. C. Green

Plate 30: 'Achilles' 3031 class 4-2-2, No. 3079 *Thunderbolt* with the 10.36a.m. 'up' express at Knowle & Dorridge on 12th June 1911. Between 1905 and 1906, the engine had been fitted with a No. 2 non-taper boiler.

H. W. Burman/C. C. Green

Plate 31: The 2-6-2 tank engine, No. 3905 was one of twenty '2301' class 0-6-0s converted between 1907 and 1910. It is pictured, on 28th August 1913, at Tyseley Shed, and was originally numbered 2499.

H. W. Burman/C. C. Green

Plate 32: A view of Earlswood Lakes station, shortly after its opening. Note the covered footbridge and the crossover road used in connection with the termination of some local push-pull or railcar units, and, for a similar purpose, the water column. Earlswood, and later The Lakes Halt, were popular weekend stations for anglers.

City of Birmingham Reference Library

Plate 33: Yardley Wood Platform, shortly after the opening of the North Warwick line as seen from the overbridge, and looking towards Bearley and Stratford-upon-Avon. The train on the right, with an 0-4-2 tank, is probably a Henley-in-Arden to Birmingham Moor Street local.

City of Birmingham Reference Library

YARDLEY WOOD PLATFORM.

Plate 34: Birmingham (Moor Street) Station, circa 1916. On the left is a typical wooden hut used by GWR ticket collectors, whilst the notices, above the railings, demand that all tickets and season tickets must be shewn here. Between these notices is the red 'penny in the slot' platform ticket machine. The platform in the picture is of the island type and a further platform is to the left, out of the photograph. The engine would be either a 2-4-0T or 0-4-2T and is standing with its wheels just off the traverser. On the right is the newly-built goods shed.

British Rail

Plate 35: The rebuilt Snow Hill Station, circa 1912 showing the main 'up' departure platform.

British Rail

Plate 36: French-built De Glehn compound 4-4-2, No. 104 *Alliance*, still retaining its original cab and boiler, stands at No. 7 platform at Snow Hill with an Oxford train, circa 1915. All engines of this class were stationed at Oxford and used on Birmingham and Wolverhampton trains from 1913 onwards.

P. B. Whitehouse Collection

Plate 37: A 1912 view of the interior of Snow Hill North signal box locking frame.

D. Harrison Collection

Plate 38: One of the 'Saint' class 4-6-0s to survive into the British Railways' era, No. 2947 *Madresfield Court,* stands at Snow Hill waiting for a northbound train, probably circa July 1912.

H. W. Burman/C. C. Green

Plate 39: No. 1047, one of the 1016 class, which were originally saddle tanks, is pictured at Snow Hill with a 'down' local train on 9th July 1912, six months after conversion. This engine was the last of its class to survive, being withdrawn in July 1935.

H. W. Burman/C. C. Green

Plate 40: Displaying its old number, 3402 (later renumbered 3702), 'City' class 4-4-0, *Halifax* waits on one of the 'down' centre tracks at Snow Hill on 9th July 1912.

H. W. Burman/C. C. Green

Plate 41: A 'Star' class 4-6-0 No. 4023 *King George,* renamed *Danish Monarch* in 1927, waits alongside No. 4 bay platform at Snow Hill on 9th July 1912. The engine was then only three years old.

H. W. Burman/C. C. Green

Plate 42:   Snow Hill Station, circa 1912. The concourse, in the foreground, had to serve as a car parking area in later years, needing the constant attention of a railway policeman to prevent blocking and overcrowding. The platform sign indicates the existence of the new North Warwick line to Stratford-upon-Avon reading 'To platforms 7, 8, 9, 10, 11 & 12 for all stations to Leamington, Oxford, Reading, London, South of England, Stratford-upon-Avon, Cheltenham, Gloucester, Bristol and West of England'. The timetable board, a frame which remained in place until the last days, is headed 'GWR: The Holiday Line' whilst its major poster, headed GWR and L&NWR displays these two railways' cheap returns to London. This competition was now possible because of the recently-opened line via Bicester and Princes Risborough, services previously being routed via Oxford. It was colloquially known as the 'Great Way Round'.

British Rail

Plate 43:   'Saint' class 4-6-0, No. 173 (later No. 2973) *Robins Bolitho* was one of the first true Churchward locomotives and was a pioneer 4-6-0 engine. It is pictured with a London bound train, about to leave Snow Hill in April 1911. Originally built without names, these early 4-6-0 locomotives were renumbered in the 29XX series in 1912.

H. W. Burman/C. C. Green

Plate 44: A scene at Hockley, in February 1911, towards the completion of the new works in the Birmingham area. The locomotive is an ex-West Midlands Railway (ex-Oxford, Worcester & Wolverhampton) 0-6-0. It is carrying the later of its two GWR numbers, 43 (formerly 264), having been Oxford, Worcester & Wolverhampton engine No. 49. Built in 1856, by E. B. Wilson, it was finally withdrawn in 1921 after a total of well over a million miles travelled, whilst in service.

H. W. Burman/C. C. Green

Plate 45: West Bromwich Station, which opened in 1854, is shown as it was around 1910. This photograph, reproduced from a local postcard, shows the signalling with standard posts and arms, first and second class (separate) ladies' and gentlemen's waiting-rooms, and the once familiar enamel advertisements. These include Stevens Ink, Typhoo Tea and Mitchells & Butlers Beers and Ales.

West Bromwich Reference Library, Metropolitan Borough of Sandwell

Tyseley Station. N^r Birmingham

Plate 46: Tyseley Station, just prior to completion, in 1906. This was shortly to become the junction for the new North Warwick line to Bearley.

City of Birmingham Reference Library

Plate 47: This photograph, taken by Lewis Lloyd, is of the construction work on the new North Warwick line near Tyseley in 1906.

City of Birmingham Reference Library

Plate 48: A further look at the construction work on the new North Warwick line near Tyseley in 1906.

City of Birmingham Reference Library

Plate 49 (below): The replacement of the original bridge girders at Small Heath, in March 1907, as part of the widening and modernization scheme, carried out, in the Birmingham area, by the GWR. Worthy of note is the Birmingham Corporation tramcar in the background.

D. Harrison Collection

Plate 50: Acocks Green Station, from an old coloured picture postcard of the turn of the century, well before the widening to Olton and the construction of the North Warwick line. Acocks Green Station would then serve the area between the existing station, built during the widening, and Tyseley, which did not exist until 1908.

P. B. Whitehouse Collection

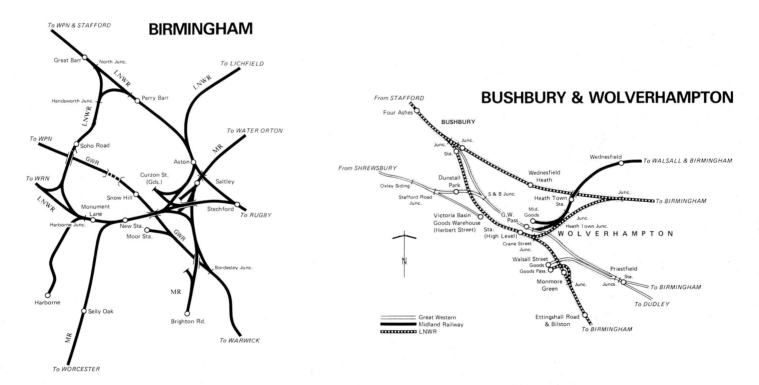

BIRMINGHAM

BUSHBURY & WOLVERHAMPTON

Plates 51 & 52:   Two scenes at Shrewsbury with 'Bulldog' class 4-4-0. No. 3402 *Jamaica*, running light engine past the junction box, and 'Beyer' 322 class outside-framed 0-6-0, No. 358 on pilot duties. No. 358 was one of a class of thirty locomotives, ordered from Beyer Peacock by Gooch and Armstrong. The first twenty of these dated from 1864 but No. 358, an Armstrong engine, was built in 1886. The photograph was taken in 1927 and the locomotive was withdrawn in 1930. All the engines in this class ran over a million miles with No. 358 reaching 1¼ million.

P. M. Alexander

Plate 53: A view of 'Bulldog' class 4-4-0, No. 3371 *Sir Massey Lopes,* taken in 1926, whilst the locomotive was negotiating the sharp curves of Rainbow Hill Junction, near Foregate Street, Worcester, with a heavy Cardiff to Birmingham train.

P. M. Alexander

Plate 54: 'City' class 4-4-0 No. 3703 *Hobart* is pictured at Leamington Spa in the 1920s. Of particular interest in this view are the racks of luggage labels on the right, at the rear of the platform.

A. W. Flowers

Plate 55: The French Atlantics were fairly frequent visitors to the Banbury, Leamington and Birmingham lines during the 1920s. This photograph was probably taken around 1925 and shows No. 102 *La France,* complete with its Swindon No. 1 boiler, alongside the 'up' platform at Leamington Spa. In the background are the tall ex-LNWR signals for LMS trains to Rugby and Daventry.

A. W. Flowers

Plate 56: No. 3819 *County of Salop*, a Churchward 'County' class 4-4-0, stands at Leamington Spa Station in 1928. It is heading a fast train from Snow Hill to Weymouth, via Oxford and Reading.

P. Hopkins

Plate 57: One of the 1902-built 2-4-2 tanks, No. 3616, simmers at Leamington Spa with a local train from Birmingham, in 1933, its last year in service. About half of this class of thirty engines worked out their lives in this area and No. 3616 had served the district since about 1910. The class was superseded by the 51XX 2-6-2 tanks.

P. Hopkins

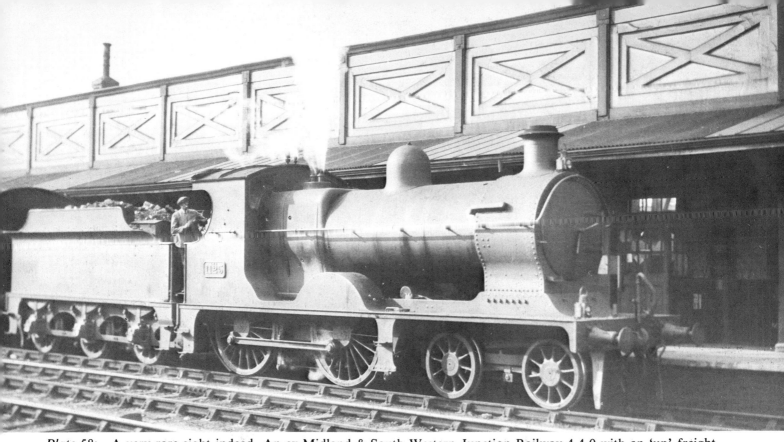

Plate 58: A very rare sight indeed. An ex-Midland & South Western Junction Railway 4-4-0 with an 'up' freight arrives at Leamington Spa in September 1929. The engine is No. 1125, and has almost certainly worked up from Cheltenham, via Stratford-upon-Avon.

P. Hopkins

Plate 59: A photograph, taken in the 1920s, of an 1869-built 2-4-0 tank, No. 457 standing at the 'down' main line platform at Leamington Spa with a train for Stratford-upon-Avon. The engine was a genuine 'Metropolitan', the condensing gear having been removed in 1883. Between 1929 and 1931, it was fitted with auto apparatus and ATC, and in 1934, the locomotive was withdrawn from service.

A. W. Flowers

Plate 60: This photograph, taken with a box camera, shows a view of Leamington Spa Station, looking south, in 1929. The footbridge access to the LMS (ex-LNWR) station was later removed and a new connection was made by subway. On the left are tracks running off to join the LMS line, whilst in the background are the buildings of the LMS station. The LMS, from Leamington Spa, served the town of Kenilworth and the cities of Coventry and Birmingham, and also the branches to Rugby and Daventry on the West Coast Main Line. Whilst a suburban set stands on one of the middle roads, a 43XX class 2-6-0, as station pilot, waits with two through coaches from Stratford-upon-Avon which will be attached to an 'up' express.

P. Hopkins

Plate 61: A 'down' London (Paddington) to Birmingham (Snow Hill) and Wolverhampton (Low Level) express speeds over Rowington Troughs. The locomotive is No. 6017 *King Edward VI* and the photograph was taken towards the end of the 1920s soon after the 'Kings' were built.

P. B. Whitehouse Collection

Plate 62: A 'Star' class 4-6-0, No. 4041 *Prince of Wales* with a short four coach 'up' express takes on water at Rowington Troughs, probably in the mid-1920s.

P. B. Whitehouse Collection

Plate 63: A 'down' express, probably during the 1920s, speeds over Rowington Troughs behind one of the 1913-built 'Stars', which were named after the sons of King George V. This is No. 4043 *Prince Henry.*

P. B. Whitehouse Collection

Plate 64: A through freight train, hauled by a 43XX class 2-6-0. approaches Knowle & Dorridge signal box and station in 1927. The tall repeating arm wooden signals were still in use. There was a small goods yard to the south of the station.

R. Carpenter Collection

Plate 65: Knowle & Dorridge (old) Station, looking towards Birmingham, in 1926. Just visible beyond the platform starter, with its small arm for calling on, is the goods loop where four tracks extended to Bentley Heath. Comparing this picture with the one taken in 1891, from the end of the 'down' platform, it can be seen that the brick-arched bridge has now been removed.

P. Hopkins

Plate 66: A Birmingham to Leamington local train, of short wheelbase stock, on the 'up' line between Bentley Heath Crossing and Knowle & Dorridge. The locomotive is an early 51XX class 2-6-2 tank probably photographed around 1920.

W. Leslie Good

Plate 67: 'County' class 4-4-0, No. 3814 *County of Chester* heads an Oxford to Birmingham, via Leamington Spa, express south of Bentley Heath during the late 1920s.

P. B. Whitehouse Collection

Plate 68: A 'down' local train of very assorted stock leaves Knowle & Dorridge behind an unidentified 'Bulldog' class 4-4-0, during the 1920s. The train is on the short section of quadruple track where goods loops ran to Bentley Heath.

W. Leslie Good

Plate:69: 'Flower' class 4-4-0, No. 4149 *Auricula* is seen between Knowle & Dorridge and Bentley Heath, prior to the 1933 quadrupling. The date is probably the mid-1920s as No. 4149 was withdrawn in 1929.

P. B. Whitehouse Collection

Plate 70: In August 1931, two 4-4-0 'Counties', both on local trains, pass near Bentley Heath. However, this scene would soon change with the new widening, and the era of the 'Counties' on express trains was virtually at an end. Clerestory coaches were also rapidly disappearing and wooden post wooden arm signals were becoming outdated. The 'up' train is headed by No 3824 *County of Cornwall*, which was withdrawn during the following month.

P. Hopkins

Plate 71: Bentley Heath Crossing signal box, circa 1926.

P. Hopkins

Plate 72: An 'up' express, possibly of the early to mid-1920s, passes between Widney Manor and Bentley Heath, behind an unidentified 'Star' class 4-6-0 locomotive.

P. B. Whitehouse Collection

Plate 73:   Widney Manor Station in the 1920s.

P. Hopkins

Plate 74: An 'Aberdare' class outside-framed 2-6-0, No. 2632, with a long train of empty stock, passes through Widney Manor (old) Station during the spring of 1931.

P. Hopkins

Plate 75: Solihull (old) signal box during its last days.

P. Hopkins

Plate 76: Solihull (old) Station, soon to become two modern island platforms approached by a passenger subway. Worthy of note are the wooden buildings on the platform and the beautifully ornate lamp standards. The view, photographed in 1926, is looking towards Leamington.

P. Hopkins

Plate 77: Olton Station, looking towards Birmingham, and photographed in 1926. The bracket signal for the 'down' relief line can clearly be seen at the end of the platform.

P. Hopkins

Plate 78: The interior of Moor Street Goods Depot in the early days of the Grouping. This depot was opened in January 1914 and handled all traffic, with the exception of livestock, that was formerly dealt with at Bordesley.
National Railway Museum

Plate 79: A 39XX class 2-6-2 tank, No. 3920 waits with a train of empty close-coupled stock on the 'up' centre road at Snow Hill, circa 1925.

A. W. Flowers

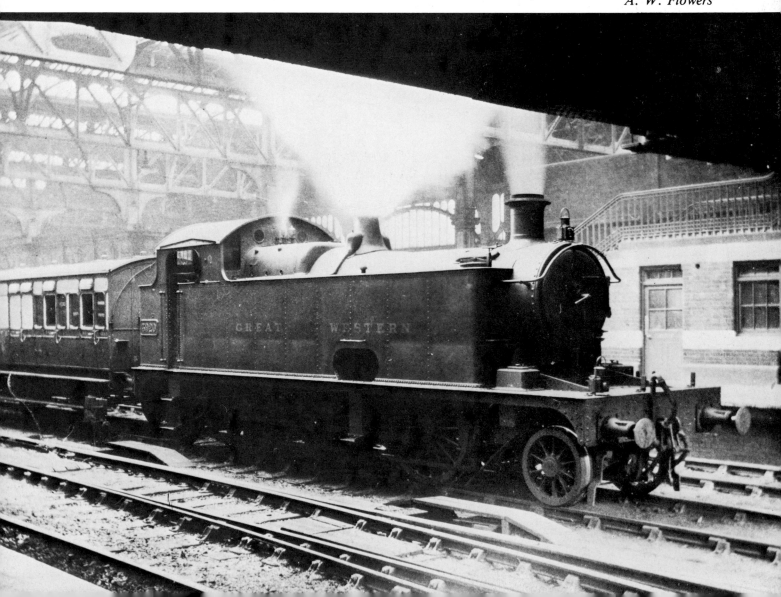

Plate 80: No. 3904, a 39XX class 2-6-2 tank engine, stands on the northbound centre track at Snow Hill, with a freight train, during the mid-1920s. These engines were converted from the 2301 class 0-6-0s in the early 1900s, (No. 3904 in 1907 from No. 2504), to satisfy a demand for more powerful suburban tanks in the Birmingham area. The 45XX class tank engine boilers were used. After 1929, they were superseded by the new 51XX class 2-6-2 tank engines. No. 3904 was withdrawn in 1933. In the background is 'Flower' class 4-4-0, No. 4149 *Auricula*.

P. B. Whitehouse Collection

Plate 81: A 3521 class 4-4-0, No. 3529 is pictured at Snow Hill in the late 1920s. This engine was built in 1877, as an 0-4-2 side tank, was rebuilt in 1891 as an 0-4-4 tank and converted, around 1899, to a 4-4-0 tender engine.

P. B. Whitehouse Collection

Plate 82: A Birmingham and South Wales express, hauled by 'County' class 4-4-0, No. 3804 *County Dublin,* and photographed in 1925.

R. Carpenter Collection

Plate 83: Snow Hill Station, looking north, in 1927, with 'Star' class 4-6-0, No. 4033 *Queen Victoria* arriving with a London express. The photograph is taken from the 'down' main line platform and the north signal box, standing on stilts, can be clearly seen.

R. Carpenter Collection

Plate 86:   Societé Alsacienne-built De Glehn compound, No. 104 *Alliance*, shown here in its final form, with a No. 1 type boiler and copper-capped chimney, at Wolverhampton (Low Level) Station, in 1925. This engine carried no name until 1907 and was withdrawn from service in 1928.

R. Carpenter Collection

Plate 87:   One of the 1910 batch of the 45XX class locomotives, with the straight-sided tanks, No. 4528, waits to pick up a local train in Wolverhampton (Low Level) Station in 1925. Immediately to the left of the locomotive, on the platform, is one of the GWR's show cases depicting interesting tourist spots served by the Great Western Railway.

R. Carpenter Collection

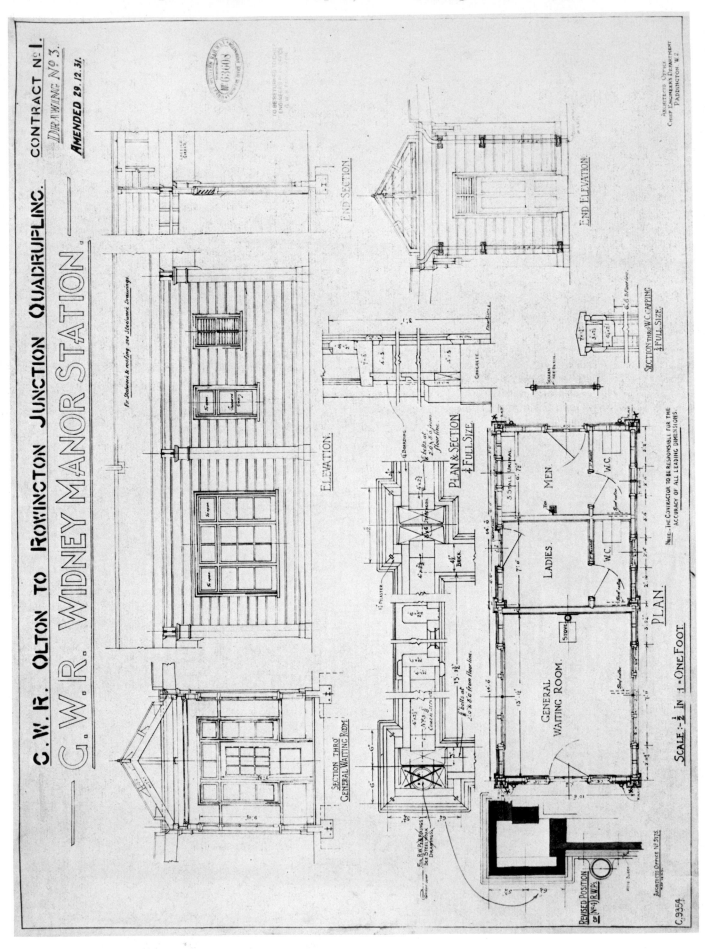

G.W.R. OLTON TO ROWINGTON JUNCTION QUADRUPLING.   CONTRACT N° I.

G.W.R. WIDNEY MANOR STATION.

DRAWING N° 3.

AMENDED 29.12.31.

ARCHITECTS OFFICE
CHIEF ENGINEER'S DEPARTMENT
PADDINGTON. W.2.

END SECTION.

END ELEVATION.

ELEVATION.

SECTION THRO' W.C. CAPPING.
½ FULL SIZE.

PLAN & SECTION
½ FULL SIZE.

SECTION THRO'
GENERAL WAITING ROOM.

MEN

LADIES.

W.C.

W.C.

GENERAL
WAITING ROOM.

PLAN.

SCALE :- ½ IN = ONE FOOT.

NOTE. THE CONTRACTOR TO BE RESPONSIBLE FOR THE
ACCURACY OF ALL LEADING DIMENSIONS.

REVISED POSITION
OF N°4 R.W.P.

C.9354.

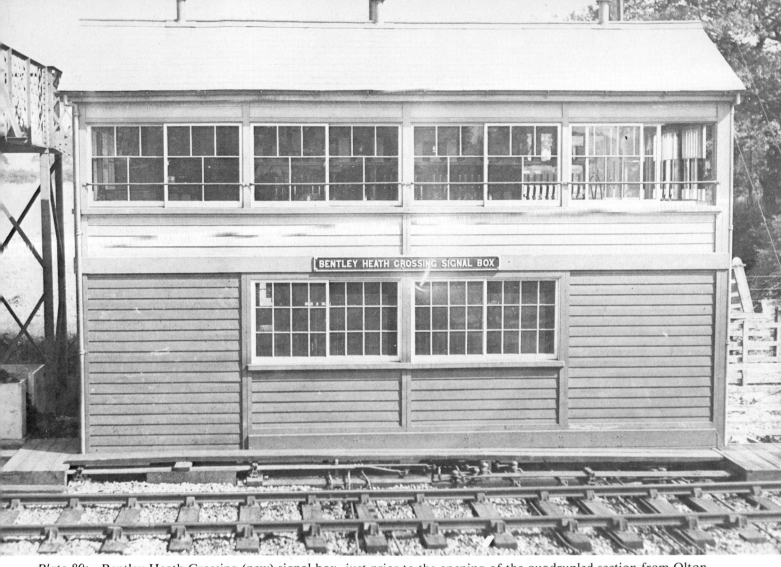

Plate 89: Bentley Heath Crossing (new) signal box, just prior to the opening of the quadrupled section from Olton to Lapworth, in 1933.
P. Hopkins

Plate 88 (left): Financed in part by an Unemployment Relief Scheme, the Great Western set about quadrupling its tracks between Olton and Lapworth during the period 1932 to 1934. The provision of these relief lines (now taken up) eased the traffic flow and enabled an excellent suburban service from Snow Hill to Leamington Spa to operate to time, as well as giving space to the numerous iron-ore freights from Banbury to Stewarts & Lloyds, Bilston. Five stations, Olton, Solihull, Widney Manor, Knowle and Lapworth were all rebuilt to modern standards and new signalling was installed throughout. This drawing shows the work put out for tender in respect of Widney Manor (new) station. The date is 29th December 1931.

City of Birmingham Reference Library

Plate 90: With the new tracks in place, but not yet ballasted, No. 6019 *King Henry V* is seen approaching Knowle & Dorridge with a Leamington Spa and London express in the late summer of 1933.
P. Hopkins

Plate 91: The new bridge for the relief lines, looking from the end of the 'down' platform at Widney Manor, as seen during the winter of 1932/3.

P. Hopkins

Plate 92: Widney Manor (old) Station, looking towards Birmingham, and photographed from the footbridge. Excavation work for the new relief lines can be seen on the left-hand side, beyond the platform, and the scene was captured in the late summer of 1932.

P. Hopkins

Plate 93: A 'R.O.D.' class 2-8-0. No. 3001, in very clean condition, takes a fast freight through Bentley Heath in the summer of 1933. Some wagons seem to be heading for Banbury and the ex-GC line as the first five are NE vehicles. The eleventh wagon appears to carry a container.

P. Hopkins

Plate 94: An engineer's train, headed by 'Duke' class 4-4-0, No. 3252 *Duke of Cornwall* is seen at Knowle & Dorridge, during the summer of 1933.

P. Hopkins

Plate 95: During two weekends in March 1934, bridge tests, over the new relief lines of the quadrupling, were conducted by the Civil Engineers. These were carried out by running four 'Kings', two coupled together, on parallel tracks at varying speeds up to 60m.p.h. This scene shows the second speed test, on 25th March 1934, at Widney Lane. Note the deflection rods being held beneath the bridge.

P. B. Whitehouse Collection

Plate 96 (below): Waiting for the 'right away', at Olton Station, during the second speed test on 25th March 1934. The leading locomotive is No. 6001 *King Edward VII* and the driver is the late George Holland who retired, in the 1960s, as a headquarters locomotive inspector.

P. B. Whitehouse Collection

Plate 97: The four 'Kings' about to carry out bridge testing at Widney Lane on 25th March 1934. The two pairs of engines first coasted across at walking pace whilst deflections were measured. This was carried out twice and the locomotives then ran back about three quarters of

a mile accelerating at speed. The normal test conditions were 500 tons in weight and 60m.p.h. In fact, the actual figures, during the tests, were 542 tons at speeds of 59-62m.p.h. Twelve runs, in all, were made over the six double track bridges which were tested. The engines used in the tests were No. 6001 with No. 6014 and No. 6017 with No. 6005. Of these, only No. 6001 was fitted with a speed meter and the latter two locomotives double-headed a train consisting of a 3rd brake and the Divisional Engineer's Saloon.

P. B. Whitehouse Collection

Plate 98: Approaching Widney Manor, at the head of seven corridor coaches, is an unidentified 'Hall' class 4-6-0 locomotive.
P. Hopkins

Plate 99: Solihull (new) signal box, photographed during the installation of the locking frame.
P. Hopkins

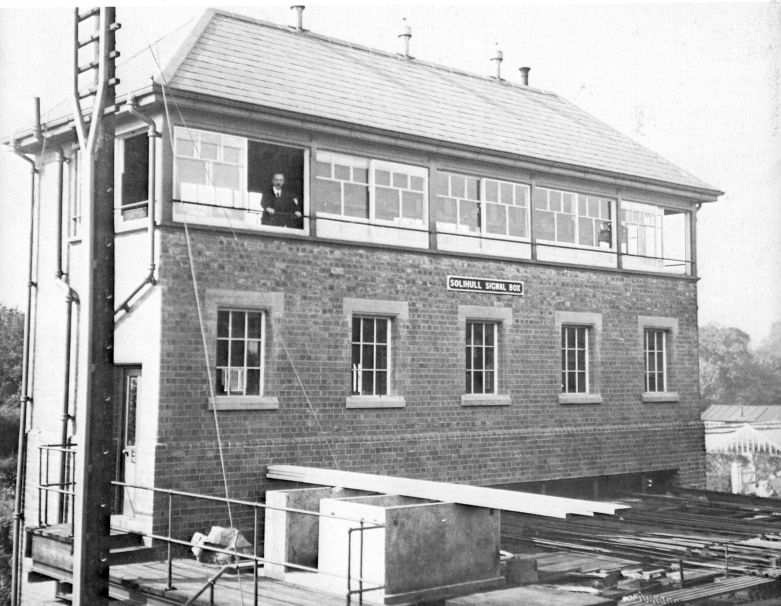

Plate 100: An experimental railcar passes Bentley Heath Crossing, circa 1933. The board at the top of the panelling reads 'Running on Michelin Pneumatic Tyres'. This was shortly before the introduction, in July 1934, of the AEC railcars on the Birmingham to Cardiff 'limited stop' service.

P. Hopkins

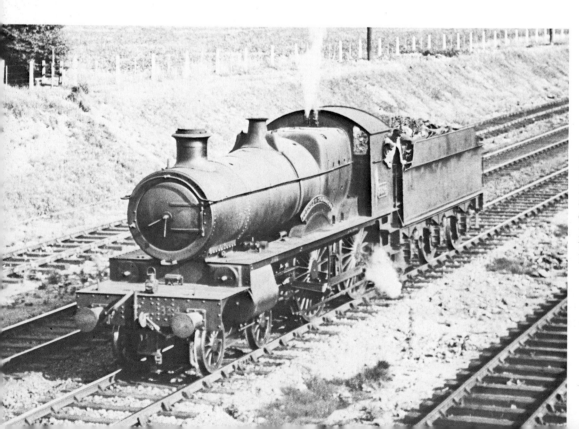

Plate 101: 'County' class 4-4-0, No. 3834 *County of Somerset* pauses at Bentley Heath in the summer of 1933. By then the class was much depleted and this particular locomotive, the last to survive, was withdrawn in November of that year.

P. Hopkins

Chapter 6 Tyseley Shed and Factory

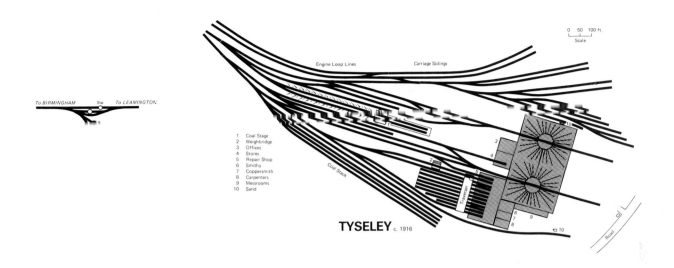

1 Coal Stage
2 Weighbridge
3 Offices
4 Stores
5 Repair Shop
6 Smithy
7 Coppersmith
8 Carpenters
9 Messrooms
10 Sand

TYSELEY c. 1916

Plate 102: A scene, photographed outside the passenger shed, at Tyseley, in 1931. In the background are the 'cripple sidings' and beyond these are the through sidings for shed access. On top of the bank, behind the clerestory coaches, is the covered carriage shed, where vehicles were cleaned by the use of power vacuums from a separate vacuum house.

R. Carpenter Collection

Plate 103: The building which housed the carriage cleaning plant at Tyseley, photographed on 4th December 1912.

British Rail

Plate 104: The carriage vacuum cleaning plant at Tyseley in 1912. An indication of the emphasis placed on passenger care and comfort.

British Rail

Plate 105: Tyseley Shed and repair shops were built in 1908 replacing an earlier shed which had been built at Bordesley. In general, the shops dealt with engines from the Birmingham Division, although Stourbridge Shed, built later, had limited facilities, and heavy general overhauls were carried out at the Stafford Road Works, at Wolverhampton. Generally, Tyseley did not handle the large passenger engines, as the London-bound expresses originated at Wolverhampton, and, over the years, the passenger locomotives at Tyseley tended to be 'Saints', 'Bulldogs', 'Dukes' and 43XX mixed traffic 2-6-0s plus a large collection of 51XX 2-6-2 tank engines. There were, in fact, at Tyseley, two shed buildings, each with a turntable, one being for passenger engines and one for freight locomotives. This scene shows Tyseley Factory at the end of GWR days. The locomotives in the factory awaiting attention include Nos. 5162 and 3033, which are seen in the foreground.

R. Carpenter Collection

Plate 106: Tyseley Junction, in the early spring of 1938, with Paddington to Birmingham and Wolverhampton express, headed by No. 6016 *King Edward V,* passing the signal box. The fireman has used his last shovelful of coal, before entering Snow Hill, and is taking it easy, prior to watching out for the Bordesley Junction distant signal, whilst the signalman and booking boy, on seeing the train's tail lamp, will give the two pause one on the bell, 'train out of section'. The arrangement of the three bracket signals controls the movements from the 'up' fast and slow lines to Leamington Spa and Stratford-upon-Avon. The tracks, to the far right of the picture, lead to the 'down' through sidings and the approach to Tyseley Shed.

P. B. Whitehouse

Plates 107 & 108 (above): At the rear of Tyseley Shed was a large area of open land adjacent to Warwick Road. It was the normal practice at weekends to store prepared engines here, and enthusiasts, not having shed permits, could gaze and number spot without being chased off. On this occasion, in 1933, one of the large 2-8-0s, No. 4705, was on view, together with 'Hall' class 4-6-0, No. 4971 *Stanway Hall*.

P. Hopkins

Plate 109 (below): 'Barnum' class 2-4-0, No. 3210 is seen on shed at Tyseley after attention in the repair shop, in 1933. This was an unusual engine for the Birmingham Division.

R. Carpenter Collection

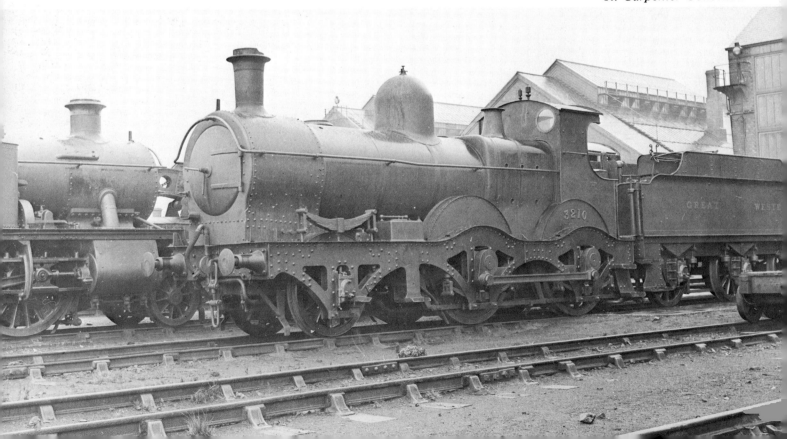

Plate 110: Inside Tyseley Shed, in 1933, is, 'Bulldog' class 4-4-0, No. 3450 *Peacock*. Used, in the main, for services on the Stratford-upon-Avon line, this engine, at times, ventured as far north-west as Barmouth, travelling by way of Ruabon and Dolgelly, on Saturday excursions.

R. Carpenter Collection

Plate 111: A visiting 'Saint', No. 2987 *Bride of Lammermoor* photographed, in the mid 1920s, inside Tyseley roundhouse.

A. W. Flowers

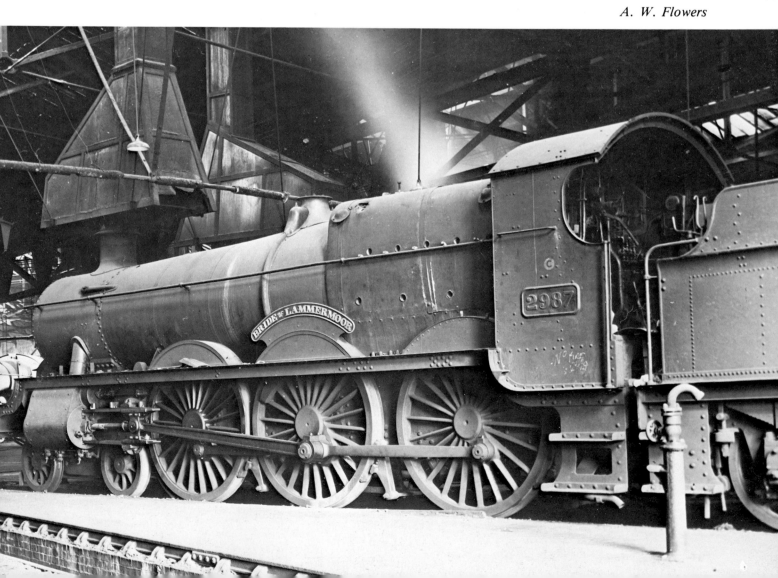

Plate 112: A Saturday check up for a new GWR diesel railcar, No. 5, at Tyseley Factory, in 1935.

F. E. Hemming

Plate 113: 'R.O.D' class 2-8-0, No. 3037 stands outside the repair shop at Tyseley.

P. B. Whitehouse Collection

Plate 114: Shed conditions after World War II were scarcely ideal as can be seen from this view of a fitter at work, in 1947.

P. B. Whitehouse

Plate 115: On shed at the same date, with its parallel chimney is 'Duke' class 4-4-0, No. 3274, originally named *Newquay*.

R. Carpenter Collection

Chapter 7 The 1930s: Birmingham to Leamington

Plate 116: Olton Station, now rebuilt on a new site, with two island platforms having boarded edges, facing the relief lines. An unidentified 'Hall' class 4-6-0, with a 3,500 gallon tender, heads a Snow Hill to Leamington Spa suburban train during 1935. The stock consists of five coaches; a clerestory corridor plus a standard Birmingham Division four coach non-corridor set.

P. B. Whitehouse

Plate 117: 'Bulldog' class 4-4-0, No. 3353 *Pershore Plum* is pictured between Bordesley Junction and Birmingham (Moor Street) stations. This photograph, of a Stratford-upon-Avon to Moor Street train, was taken from a passing Leamington to Snow Hill local in the 1930s.

F. E. Hemming

Plate 118: The fireman takes his ease as Churchward 2-8-0, No. 2878 heads a northbound freight over the double-tracked bridge near Rowington Junction in September 1931.

P. Hopkins

Plate 119: Relegated to 'all stations' locals, 'Saint' class 4-6-0, No. 2914 *Saint Augustine* waits at Widney Manor with an 'up' local, one evening in 1935.

P. Hopkins

Plate 120: Hatton Junction, in 1934, photographed from the steps of Hatton North signal box. The through lines from Birmingham to Leamington and beyond are on the left, whilst on the right is the Stratford branch, which was then, as now, a single line. The platform sign reads Hatton, junction for Bearley, Alcester & Stratford on Avon. The signals adjacent to Hatton South signal box still carry the rings on their arms indicating the slow or secondary route.

P. Hopkins

Plate 121: An 'up' express approaches Rowington Troughs, around 1934, when the 'Saints' were in use on the Birkenhead to Birmingham (Snow Hill) and South of England trains. The signal, on the left, protects the old branch to Henley-in-Arden then used as stock sidings. The train is a mixture of Great Western and Southern stock and is headed by No. 2928 *Saint Sebastian*.

P. Hopkins

Plate 122: In the late 1930s, 'King' class locomotives hauled the Wolverhampton to London expresses, but the 3p.m. ex-Snow Hill to Paddington train was at times headed by the only semi-streamlined 'Castle', No. 5005 *Manorbier Castle,* seen here approaching Leamington Spa. This engine was modified in 1935 but her hull nose feature only lasted until 1939.

F. E. Hemming

Plate 123: Warwick Station lay at the foot of one of the inevitable climbs, from the south, into Birmingham. This was the five miles of 1 in 103 and 1 in 105 to Hatton. Under normal circumstances, the run was adequate enough from Leamington for freights to have a stab at this, but one of the duties of Leamington Shed was to find a banker, which would sit at Warwick in the small bay along-side the 'down' platform. In July 1933, outside-framed 'Armstrong Goods' No. 354 was the regular banker, and it is seen at this location a month prior to with-drawal. The engine was a real veteran, dating back to 1866.

P. Hopkins

Plate 124: The 4.05p.m. semi-fast, from Birmingham Snow Hill, waits to move off from Hatton Station, in 1934, behind 'Saint' class 4-6-0 No. 2945 *Hillingdon Court.* This was soon to become a 'Star' working with Nos. 4016 *Knight of the Golden Fleece* and No. 4018 *Knight of the Grand Cross* becoming regular performers. This working was a Reading train which followed the 3.55p.m. express to Paddington, stopping at Warwick, Leamington Spa, Banbury and Oxford.

P. Hopkins

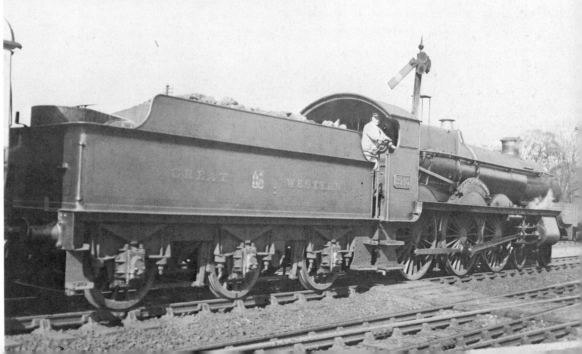

Plate 125: A view of the reconstruction of Leamington Spa Station in 1938.

R. Carpenter Collection

Plate 126: Another scene during the rebuilding in 1938. The new offices, refreshment room, etc, near completion on the 'down' platform, whilst the older wooden structure on the 'up' side is still in place. After this work was completed, the GWR stations from Leamington Spa to Birmingham were smart, clean and, where the quadrupling had taken place four years earlier, new.

R. Carpenter Collection

Plate 127: Leamington Shed on 12th February 1939. Locomotives in view include Nos. 2838, 5700 and 8100, the latter having arrived, when new, at this depot.

R. Carpenter Collection

Plate 128: A scene at Leamington Spa in 1938. A four coach non-corridor Birmingham Division set, headed by 2-6-2 tank No. 5187, enters the 'down' platform with empty stock to make up one of the 'all stations' trains to Birmingham Snow Hill and Wolverhampton (Low Level).

R. Carpenter Collection

The North Warwick line gave the Great Western a through route to Stratford-upon-Avon and beyond, avoiding the use of Hatton Junction, and providing a series of suburban stations for Birmingham commuters. The line was opened in 1908. The two junctions were at Tyseley and Bearley with the principal intermediate station being at Henley-in-Arden.

Plate 129:   Shirley Station, pictured here, had full facilities, including an overbridge, a small goods shed for pick-up freight and a platform signal box.

P. Hopkins

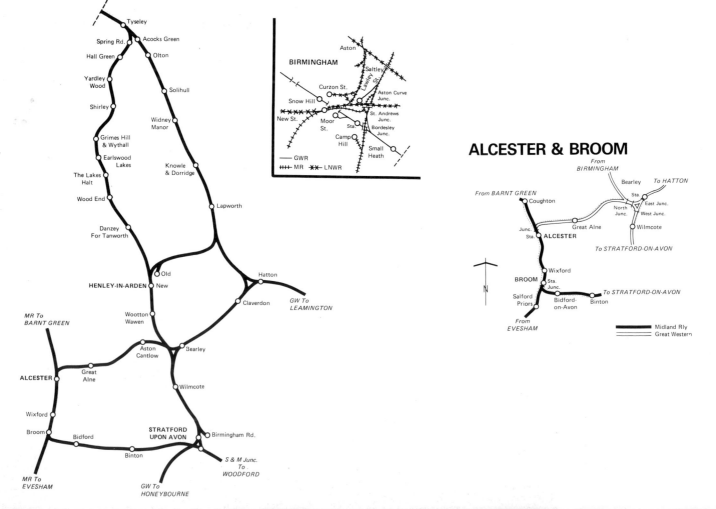

Plate 130: 'Bulldog' class 4-4-0, No. 3410 *Columbia* is pictured with a Birmingham (Snow Hill) semi-fast to Stratford-upon-Avon and Worcester in 1934. The new wide-windowed corridor stock is of particular interest.

P. B. Whitehouse Collection

Plate 131: Yardley Wood Platform, so called, as although it was manned, the passenger facilities were minimal. Access to the platforms was via the road bridge.

P. Hopkins

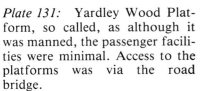

Plate 132: A new GWR railcar passes through Henley-in-Arden Station with a through express from Birmingham (Snow Hill) to Cardiff, in the late summer of 1934. This is one of the three buffet railcars and was used on this service from 9th July until wartime conditions brought it to an end in 1940. All seats were bookable and a supplement of 2/6d (12½p) was payable.

P. Hopkins

Plate 133: 'Saint' class 4-6-0, No. 2908 *Lady of Quality* is pictured near Bearley Junction in 1933. The photograph is taken from the aqueduct, where the branch engines took water, looking towards Stratford-upon-Avon. Bearley Station is out of sight to the left, and the bracket signal is off for a North Warwick train to Stratford-upon-Avon. To the right is the Alcester branch which was closed to passenger traffic in 1939, although unadvertised workmen's trains ran to Great Alne until 1944.

P. Hopkins

Plate 134: Grimes Hill and Wythall Platform, situated 5¾ miles from Tyseley, in the outer suburbs, had only a toilet, pagoda-roofed wooden waiting facilities, and a ticket-office at the top of the ramp.

P. Hopkins

Plate 135: Bearley Station, looking towards Claverdon and Leamington, in 1935. Close examination shows the two tracks merging into a single line at the far end of the platform.

P. Hopkins

Plate 136: The (old) Claverdon Station, on the branch from Hatton Junction to Bearley, where it meets the North Warwick line from Tyseley. This photograph was taken just prior to the doubling of the section and the rebuilding of the station on the opposite (south-east) side of the road bridge.

P. Hopkins

Plate 137:   Bearley South Junction, with 'Bulldog' class 4-4-0, No. 3449 *Nightingale* on a freight from Worcester to Leamington Spa via Stratford-upon-Avon. The train was photographed about 1933 when the 'Bulldog' class of locomotive was beginning to be decimated due to the construction of the new 'Hall' class 4-6-0 locomotives. The fixed distant signal, seen in this view, served the Alcester branch.

P. Hopkins

Plate 138: The branch train from Alcester approaches Bearley Junction, in this 1933 scene, behind 0-4-2T, No. 564. This locomotive was built in 1869 and was withdrawn six months after this picture was taken. The signal behind the train controls the movements on to the main line and into the station.

P. Hopkins

Plate 139: A line of wagons, stored on the closed Alcester branch, near Aston Cantlow, during World War II.

P. Hopkins

Plate 140: Aston Cantlow Halt, on the Alcester branch, photographed during 1940.

P. Hopkins

Plate 141: Beyond Stratford-upon-Avon, to the south-west, was Honeybourne Junction, deep in the heart of Worcestershire, serving as an interchange point for Cheltenham, Gloucester, Worcester, Oxford and London. This was a fascinating place to watch trains. Not only was one given the chance to see the through Paddington to Worcester and Hereford expresses, hauled by 'Stars' and 'Castles', rushing past at speed, but also the Birmingham to the West of England expresses and numerous semi-fasts and stoppers to and from Stratford-upon-Avon and Worcester via Evesham. Honeybourne Junction Station was very much a GWR country junction with its awning and pagoda-type roofs, a covered footbridge and excellent waiting facilities, but few passengers. This picture of the empty platforms, with the typical period platform trolleys, weighing machine, chocolate machines and train indicator arms, was taken in 1935. The indication on the arm pointing to the left-hand side of the island platform reads 'Stratford-upon-Avon and Leamington Spa' and the time is 10.30a.m.

P. Hopkins

Plate 142: 'Hall' class 4-6-0, No. 4918 *Dartington Hall* stands at platform 2 of Honeybourne Station with a northbound excursion from the West of England. The locomotive, still with its 3,500 gallon tender, is taking on water to ensure that the tank is full before tackling the steep climb from Stratford-upon-Avon to Bearley South Junction.

P. Hopkins

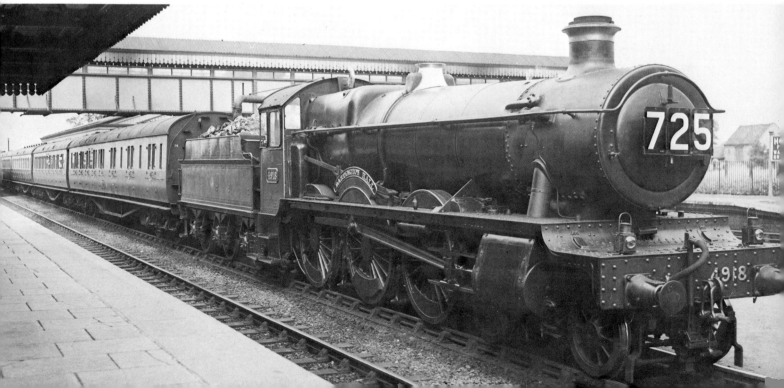

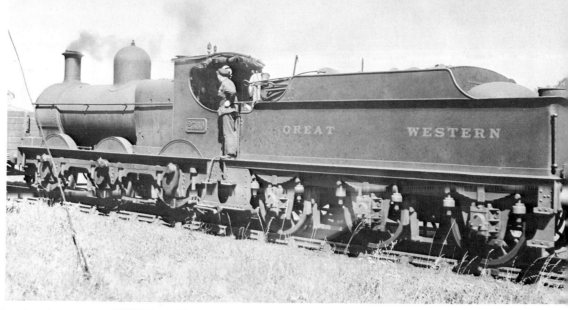

Plate 143: A Worcester-based outside-framed 2361 class 0-6-0, No. 2380 pictured, during 1935, at Honeybourne Junction.

P. Hopkins

Plate 144: A through freight approaches platform 4 behind Churchward 2-8-0, No. 2824, during 1935.

P. Hopkins

Plate 145: 'Star' class 4-6-0, No. 4049 *Princess Maud* waits at Honeybourne Junction, with an excursion train for the West of England from Stourbridge Junction, on a summer Saturday in August 1935.

P. Hopkins

Plate 146: Shipston on Stour Station - the terminus of the branch which ran from Moreton-in-Marsh, photographed during September 1931.

P. Hopkins

Plate 147: Just out of period, but complimentary to the above photograph, is this picture of the opposite end of the Shipston on Stour branch, at Moreton-in-Marsh. The photograph shows ex-Midland & South Western Junction Railway 2-4-0, No. 1335, about to leave with a Stephenson Locomotive Society special in August 1952. At that time the branch was still open for the occasional freight worked by a 'Dean Goods' 0-6-0 locomotive.

P. B. Whitehouse

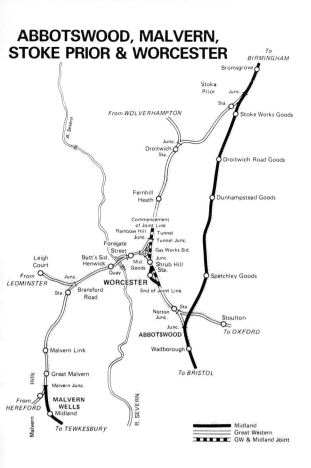

ABBOTSWOOD, MALVERN, STOKE PRIOR & WORCESTER

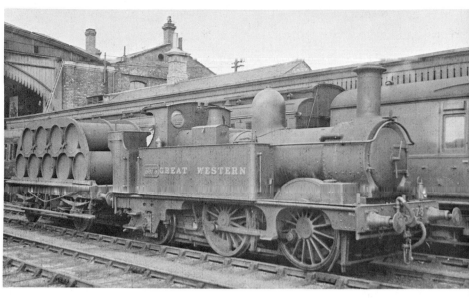

Plate 148: Worcester (Shrub Hill) Station, with 0-4-2 tank No. 3573, built 1895, operating as station pilot, during 1933.

P. Hopkins

Plate 149: A view of the Great Western engine shed at Evesham, looking towards Worcester. The engine on the left of the picture appears to be 'Dean Goods' No. 2537 and the one on the right, is 45XX 2-6-2 tank, No. 4558.

W. A. Camwell

Plate 150: A 51XX class 2-6-2 tank, No. 5102, waits in one of the north departure bay platforms at Snow Hill at the head of a train of clerestory stock, circa 1929/30.

A. W. Flowers

Plate 151: Snow Hill Station, in August 1939, with a 'Hall' class 4-6-0 heading the 9.45a.m. (SO) through train to Cardiff, Tenby and Pembroke Dock, stopping en route at Stourbridge Junction, Hagley, Kidderminster, Droitwich, Worcester (Foregate Street) and Hereford.

F. E. Hemming

Plate 152: 'Saint' class 4-6-0, No. 2903 *Lady of Lyons*, a Tyseley engine, as can be seen from the stencilled shed code, (TYS) on running plate, acts as station pilot at Snow Hill. During the late 1930s, this was a regular duty for this class of locomotive, often interspersed with local trips to Leamington Spa. The engine is attaching a six-wheeled tank wagon to the rear of an express which is heading south.

P. B. Whitehouse Collection

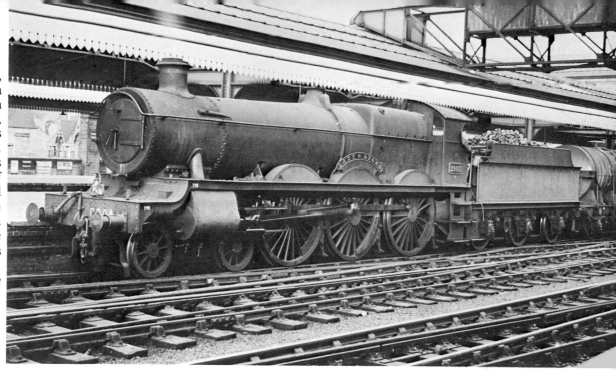

Plate 154: A Snow Hill to Wolverhampton local at Soho & Winson Green Station in the 1930s. At this time, the 51XX 2-6-2 tanks were well established on these services. They were very much masters of the job as is clear by the wisp of steam from the safety valve, as the fireman looks back down the platform and awaits for the 'right away'.

F. E. Hemming

Plate 153: The Birmingham (Snow Hill) to Dudley (via Swan Village) local services were mostly push-pull steam trains, prior to the use of GWR railcars. The 64XX was on duty on this occasion in 1936.

F. E. Hemming

Plate 155: 'Bulldog' class 4-4-0, No. 3399 *Ottawa* approches Snow Hill Station, from the north, with an express for Stratford-upon-Avon and beyond, during the summer of 1936. Behind the train is the covered water tank and the turntable.

P. B. Whitehouse

Plates 156 to 158 (below & opposite): Three engines are pictured in the vicinity of Snow Hill turntable, during 1932. The two 'bulldogs' are Nos. 3327 *Marco Polo* and 3353 *Pershore Plum,* a very local name which replaced its old name *Plymouth* in 1927. *Pershore Plum* regularly hauled the so-called Birmingham and South Wales Express, which stopped at Smethwick Junction, Stourbridge Junction, Kidderminster, Worcester (Foregate Street) and stations to Hereford and Newport. The 'Star' is No. 4039 *Queen Matilda.*

A. W. Flowers

Plate 159: Cleobury Mortimer Station with ex-CMDP Manning Wardle 0-6-0 tank, No. 29, at one time named *Burwarton* pictured with a Ditton Priors train in the branch platform. This line was absorbed by the GWR at the Grouping and its two saddle tanks were rebuilt as pannier tanks in 1924 (No. 29) and 1931 (No. 28). No. 28 lasted until 1953 and No. 29 until 1954.

F. E. Hemming

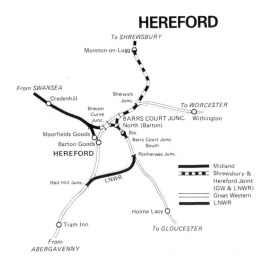

HEREFORD

To SHREWSBURY
Moreton-on-Lugg

From SWANSEA
Credenhill

Shelwick Junc.
Brecon Curve Junc.
BARRS COURT JUNC.   To WORCESTER
North (Barton)   Withington

Moorfields Goods
Sta.
Barton Goods   Barrs Court Junc. South
HEREFORD
Rotherwas Junc.

Red Hill Junc.   LNWR

	Midland
	Shrewsbury & Hereford Joint (GW & LNWR)
	Great Western
	LNWR

Holme Lacy
Tram Inn   To GLOUCESTER
From ABERGAVENNY

Plate 160 (above right): Hereford Shed on 11th April 1937. In the yard stand 43XX class 2-6-0s Nos. 5345 and 5355 and under the sheer legs (GWR sheds did not use wheel drops), is ex-'R.O.D.' 2-8-0, No. 3038.

P. M. Alexander

Plate 161 (below right): Double-framed 2361 class 0-6-0, No. 2380, built in 1886, stands outside Worcester Shed, sometime during 1930. Unlike the 'Dean Goods' 0-6-0s, these engines were rarely seen on passenger trains. Nos. 2362 and 2380 were originally withdrawn in 1939, but due to wartime shortages, certain locomotives were reinstated, some being sent to the Cambrian Section at Oswestry. No. 2380 survived until 1943 and No. 2362 until 1946.

P. M. Alexander

Plate 162: Ross-on-Wye Shed on 30th July 1939. Inside the building was 0-4-2 tank, No. 4863 together with 0-6-0 pannier tank No. 7416.

W. A. Camwell

Plate 163: Much Wenlock Shed on 28th June 1936. The branch was the home for the 44XX class 2-6-2 tanks. Outside the shed is No. 4403 and inside No. 4401. Nos. 4400/6/9 were at Wellington (Salop).

W. A. Camwell

Plate 164: Ketley Station, on the Wellington to Craven Arms branch, which ran via Buildwas, as seen in September 1947. The train is the 3.05p.m. from Wellington to Much Wenlock hauled by 44XX class small-wheeled 2-6-2 tank, No. 4406.

W. A. Camwell

Plate 165: On the very fringe of the West Midlands, the 'Barnum' class 2-4-0s worked the Wellington to Crewe branch. Built in 1889 as secondary express engines, the class was relegated to branch work after World War I. The Wellington to Crewe turn was their final duty. This view, showing No. 3216, was taken around 1928, and the coaches are part of Wellington and Crewe No. 1 set. The scene is Crewe Station. Nos. 3210 and 3222 lasted until 1937.

A. W. Flowers

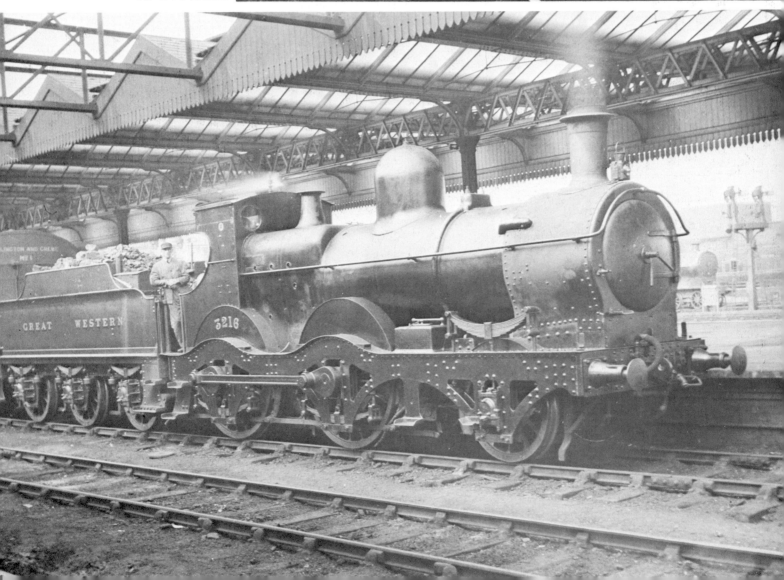

Plate 166: One of the early 'Hall' class 4-6-0s, No. 4906 *Bradfield Hall* backs on to one of the high-wheeled double-framed 4-4-0s outside Wolverhampton Stafford Road Works in the late 1920s.

A. W. Flowers

Plate 167: 'Aberdare' class outside-framed 2-6-0, No. 2679, complete with large R.O.D. tender, is seen at Oxley Shed, Wolverhampton in October 1938. A sign of the usage made by private owners, in those days, is the train of wagons, belonging to Pwllheli Granite Company Limited, on the freight train beyond the shed yard.

P. M. Alexander

Plates 168 to 170: Inside the erecting shop at the reconstructed Stafford Road Works, Wolverhampton in 1935. These three photographs clearly show the extent of the work carried out. The locomotives which are receiving attention include Nos. 5122, 4539 and 2110. No. 5122 was one of the earlier 3150 class 2-6-2 tanks which was rebuilt, between 1928 and 1930, to conform to the 51XX series.

A. W. Flowers

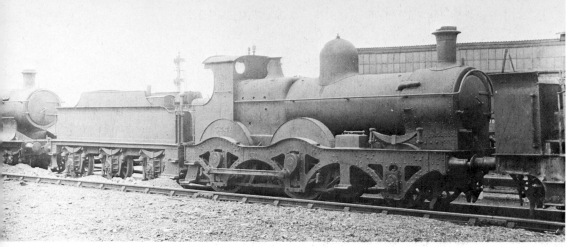

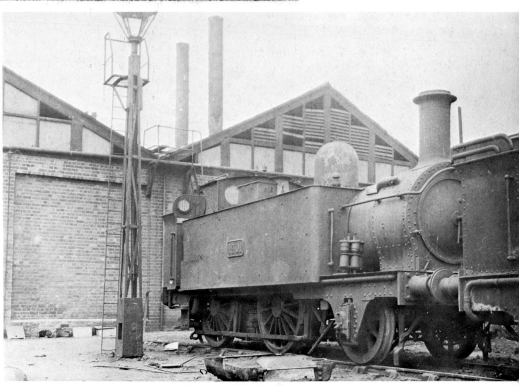

Plate 171: Outside-framed 2-4-0 No 3221 awaits attention outside Stafford Road Works, Wolverhampton in 193... This engine was a regular performer on the Wellington to Crewe line during that period.

A. W. Flowers

Plate 172: No. 1401, an open cab 'Metropolitan' 2-4-0 tank, built in 1878, stands outside Stafford Road Works, Wolverhampton, in 1932. During the last few years of its life this was one of the auto-fitted engines, and it was withdrawn in 1934.

A. W. Flowers

Plate 173: 'Metropolitan' 2-4-0T, No 3562 was still in use until 1949 and is seen inside Wolverhampton (Stafford Road) running shed in 1937.

P. B. Whitehouse

Plate 174:   Bordesley Junction, looking towards Birmingham (Moor Street) and Birmingham (Snow Hill) with the spur to the unfinished viaduct and cattle dock seen on the right of the picture. To the left are the 'down' and 'up' relief and fast lines leading to Snow Hill.

P. B. Whitehouse Collection

Plate 175:   The distant signal is on, as a precaution whilst a very grimy 'Saint', No. 2902 *Lady of the Lake* takes a stopper from the 'up' relief to the 'up' fast at Bentley Heath.   The scene is photographed just prior to nationalization and the rear coaches of the semi-fast train appear as dirty as the engine, which was one of the last of the class to survive. No. 2902 was withdrawn in 1949.

C. F. H. Oldham

Plate 176: No. 4924 *Eydon Hall* climbs Hatton Bank, towards the summit, in the summer of 1946.
R. Carpenter Collection

Plate 177: Hatton Station, looking south, photographed from the road bridge in the summer of 1947. The train in the platform is a Stratford-upon-Avon local hauled by 'Bulldog' class 4-4-0, No. 3377, which, prior to 1930, was named *Penzance*. It is an unusual scene as the train is made up of one auto- coach and is in the main line 'down' platform.

P. B. Whitehouse

Plate 178: A 51XX class 2-6-2 tank, No. 5163, with a train of Birmingham Division suburban stock, nears the summit of Hatton Bank in the spring of 1940. The train is an 'all stations' local to Birmingham (Snow Hill) from Leamington Spa and the coaches are of the old wooden-bodied snap handled type. The engine carries the almost standard GWR stopping train head-code of a single lamp, situated in the centre of the buffer beam. The distant signal is on, almost certainly indicating that a Stratford-upon-Avon train is due at Hatton Junction with a fouling movement for the main line.

P. B. Whitehouse

Plate 179: 'King' class 4-6-0, No. 6008 *King James II* approaches Hatton Junction with a 'down' Birmingham, Wolverhampton and Birkenhead train, in the spring of 1940. The right-hand track is a freight only line, which was put in approximately a third of the way down the bank to avoid delays with the slow moving and often heavy goods trains.

P. B. Whitehouse

Plate 180: A 'down' freight nears the summit of Hatton Bank, in 1947, using the freight only relief line. The train is hauled by 'Hall' class 4-6-0, No. 5944 *Ickenham Hall* and the banker is a Leamington-allocated 2-6-2 tank.

P. B. Whitehouse

Plate 181: Leamington Spa was the pick-up point for passengers in the South-East Midlands, as far as the Paddington expresses were concerned. Coventry was well served by the LMS, but the growing outer Birmingham suburban area ensured that the single stop, at Leamington Spa, for the London expresses, was both popular and profitable. In the last year of the GWR, No. 6007 *King William III* pauses with an 'up' express during the period when the timing was downgraded and stops were made at Banbury and High Wycombe.

A. W. Flowers

Plate 182: A Churchward 2-8-0, No. 2833, takes a through freight to Bordesley Junction, past the Hatton South distant signal, in the spring of 1940, with comparative ease and a full head of steam.

P. B. Whitehouse

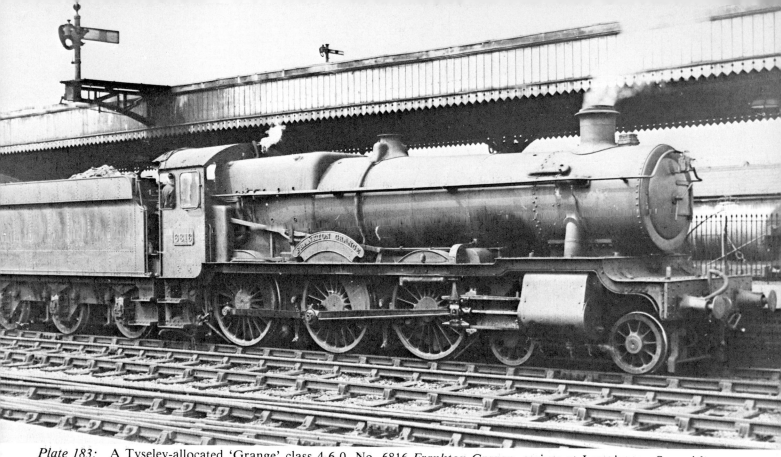

Plate 183: A Tyseley-allocated 'Grange' class 4-6-0, No. 6816 *Frankton Grange*, arrives at Leamington Spa with a local train from Birmingham (Snow Hill) in 1947.

Plate 184: The return working of one of the frequent iron-ore trains from Banbury to Stewarts & Lloyds, Bilston, pictured at Leamington Spa in 1947. These trains, sometimes worked by 28XX class 2-8-0s, were usually in the hands of these large 72XX class 2-8-2 tanks as in this scene, showing No. 7236 hauling an 'up' train with a load of coal for Banbury exchange sidings.

A. W. Flowers

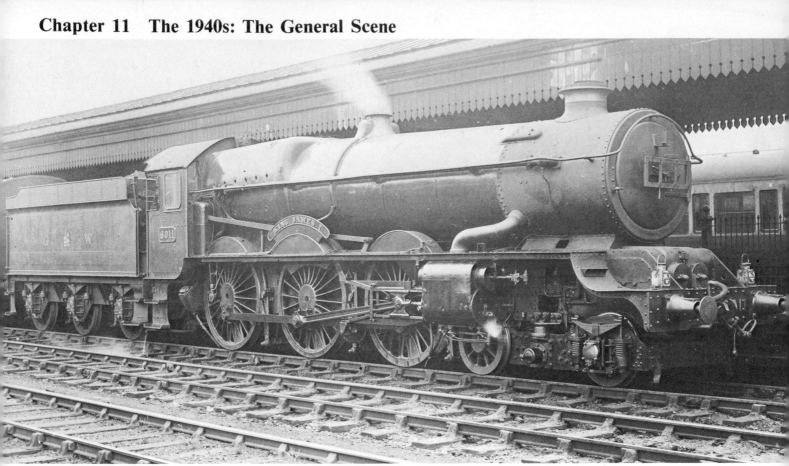

Plate 185:   A London to Birmingham and Wolverhampton express stands, in 1947, at the far end of the 'down' platform at Snow Hill. The locomotive is No. 6011 *King James I* of Stafford Road Shed, as indicated by the letters SRD seen adjacent to the buffer beam. Note the later type lettering on the tender and the speed recorder below the rear driving wheel splasher. At this time, there was an acute coal shortage and the quality of the fuel on the tender seems poor.

A. W. Flowers

Plate 186:   An unidentified 'Hall' class 4-6-0 approaches Birmingham (Moor Street) Station and Snow Hill Tunnel, with a passenger train, over the viaduct section from Bordesley Junction, just after the railways were nationalized.

P. B. Whitehouse Collection

Plate 187: The end of the platform and the signal box at Oldbury & Langley Green, photographed during the last days of GWR ownership. On the left is the freight only branch to Oldbury, which was closed to passenger traffic in 1915. Until 1936, this junction was originally named Langley Green & Rood End.

W. A. Camwell

Plate 188: An unusual suburban rush hour working. Marked with an 'X' in the timetable, indicating one class only, this Birmingham to Dudley service was GWR railcar-operated during 1947. The photograph shows the 4.35p.m. Birmingham (Snow Hill) to Dudley train at Great Bridge (GW) Station. This service, arriving at Dudley at 5p.m., ran partly over ex-LNWR metals from Horsefield Junction, through Dudley Port (Low Level) Station and on to Dudley (Great Western).

W. A. Camwell

Plate 189: A through West of England to Birmingham and Wolverhampton express approaches Stratford-upon-Avon, from Cheltenham, headed by No. 2924 *Saint Helena.* The location is near the S & M Junction signal box, a reminder of the defunct Stratford & Moreton Tramway. Looking at the grime and the heavily-loaded ten coach train, the date would seem to be around 1947.

C. F. H. Oldham

Plate 190: An unidentified, un-named 'Bulldog' class 4-4-0 nears the summit of Hatton Bank with a Stratford-upon-Avon local in 1947. Just visible, under the arch on the right of the bridge, is the Hatton Junction distant signal in the on position. This would be a precaution as the train will have to divert from the main line to the branch platform. During this period, the Hatton to Bearley section was double-tracked.

P. M. Alexander

Plate 191: Hatton Junction, probably around 1947, with 'Bulldog' class 4-4-0, No. 3447 *Jackdaw* heading a Leamington Spa to Stratford-upon-Avon local.

P. B. Whitehouse Collection

Plate 192: Un-named 'Bulldog' class 4-4-0, No. 3377 leaves Stratford-upon-Avon for Leamington Spa. The train comprises a four coach Birmingham Division set and is likely to have come from Worcester. Stratford-upon-Avon is at the foot of a formidable climb to Bearley Junction and a shed was provided for use of bankers as well as for the Birmingham suburban engines, usually 51XX 2-6-2 tanks.

P. M. Alexander

Plate 193: Droitwich, in the summer of 1946. On the left is 'Aberdare' class 2-6-0, No. 2620 with a freight from Stourbridge Junction yards. The signalman has been quick off the mark as the home signal is already back to danger. On the right is the ex-Midland Railway line from Stoke Works Junction to Worcester.

P. B. Whitehouse

Plate 194: This view of 'Aberdare' class 2-6-0, No. 2620 clearly shows the use of the ex-'R.O.D'. Great Central type tender. Note the Great Western bracket signal which still has its wooden posts.

P. B. Whitehouse

Plate 195: The southern end of Hereford (Barrs Court) Station in 1947 with 'Saint' class 4-6-0, No. 2948 *Stackpole Court,* heading a Newport train.

P. M. Alexander

Plate 196: 'Star' class 4-6-0, No. 4039 *Queen Matilda* is being prepared at Hereford Shed, on 6th November 1947, for a Cardiff train. The engine is in its almost original condition, without outside steam pipes.

P. M. Alexander

Plate 197: Hereford Shed in 1937. Coaled and ready for the road is 'Saint' class 4-6-0, No. 2987 *Bride of Lammermoor*.

P. M. Alexander

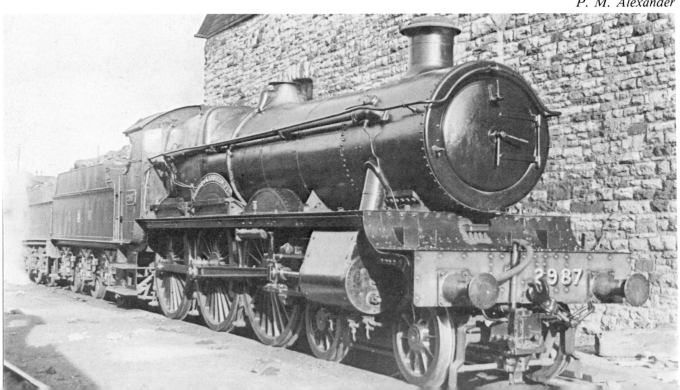

Plate 198: Truthfully, rather far north for the content of this book, but at the northern end of the Great Western's Arm reaching beyond Shrewsbury, Chester was very much on the route of the London, Birmingham to Birkenhead expresses although these were really semi-fasts beyond Wolverhampton. A 63XX 2-6-0 takes a fast freight out of the tunnels: every inch a Great Western Engine.

Eric Treacy

Plate 199: Waiting beneath a tall chimney, a 44XX class 2-6-2 tank heads a Wellington-bound train in July 1947. Both the arms of the bracket signal are at danger as the junction will shortly be crossed by a Severn Valley train.

P. B. Whitehouse

Plate 200 (below): In Great Western days, Buildwas, in Shropshire, with its huge power-station, seen in the background, was a junction for trains on the Severn Valley line from Bewdley to Bridgnorth, the branch from Wellington to Craven Arms, and also the branch to Shifnal. In 1947, the main passenger motive power was in the hands of 51XX and 45XX 2-6-2 tanks although the 44XX class were seen on the Craven Arms section. For the locomotive enthusiast, however, there was very little variety but, with the power-station coal trains arriving and leaving, this was a busy location. A Severn Valley train is seen leaving Buildwas, in July 1947, behind newly-built 51XX class 2-6-2 tank No. 4110.

P. B. Whitehouse

Plate 201: A 2021 class 0-6-0 pannier tank, built in 1904, a saddle tank until 1922, is pictured at Wellington around 1946. The engine shed is in the background and the pannier tanks were probably, at that time, used to shunt the Lilleshall Iron Works yard.

P. B. Whitehouse Collection

Plate 202: One of the few 1901 class 0-6-0 saddle tanks, which were built in 1892, that were not eventually fitted with panniers. No. 2007 shunts, at Worcester, during the summer of 1947. Even at this late stage, this was very much a Great Western yard scene of fifty years previous, with the unrebuilt engine, with its open cab, and the ubiquitous shunter's truck. No. 2007 survived into British Railways' days and was withdrawn in 1949.

P. B. Whitehouse

Plate 203:   A Halesowen Railway mile post, marking the distance from Halesowen Junction, on the main Midland Railway route from Birmingham to Bristol.

P. B. Whitehouse

HALESOWEN & NORTHFIELD

GW & Midland Joint
Great Western
Midland Rly

Plate 204 (top right):   Halesowen Station, circa 1908. Behind the bridge is the Halesowen Railway, jointly vested in the Great Western and Midland railways from 30th June 1906. The Midland ran the passenger services to King's Norton until 1919 and the Great Western trains came down from Old Hill on the Birmingham to Stourbridge Junction line, ceasing on 5th December 1927. Work-men's trains, for the Austin Factory, ran until the line's final closure.

R. Chester Lamb Collection

Plate 205 (bottom right):   An evening workmen's train leaves Longbridge for Old Hill headed by 1813 class open cab pannier, No. 1835. The stock was non-corridor and included vehicles from the standard Birmingham Division suburban sets and a clerestory coach. The scene was probably photographed between 1946 and 1947.

P. B. Whitehouse Collection

Plate 206: Wolverhampton-built 655 class 0-6-0 pannier tank, No. 1745 runs bunker first over Dowery Dell Viaduct with the Longbridge-bound empty stock for the evening workmen's train, in the summer of 1947, shortly before the 64XX class locomotives took over this service.

P. B. Whitehouse

Plate 207: Swindon-built 1813 class pannier tank, No. 1835 waits in the platform at Rubery with the second empty stock train for Longbridge on the same evening. At this point, it will pass No. 1745 which will be hauling a train to Old Hill, the second platform face at Longbridge being occupied by the LMS train for Birmingham (New Street).

P. B. Whitehouse

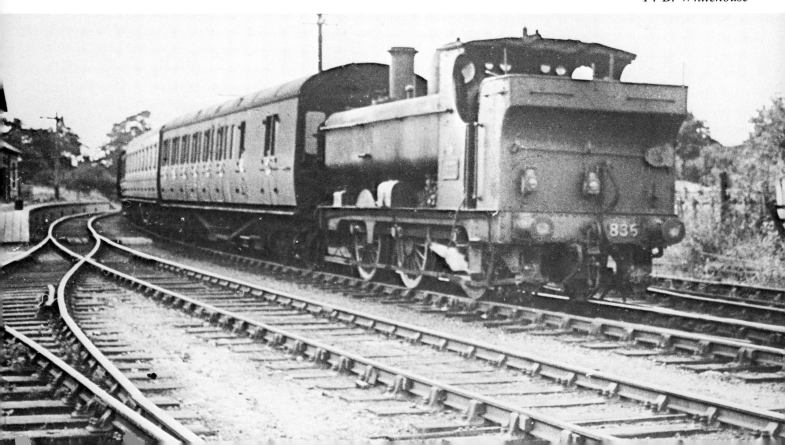

Plate 208: A Longbridge to Old Hill branch train nears Hunnington, behind a 64XX class 0-6-0 pannier tank. This was one of two evening workmen's trains serving the Austin Works; both were unadvertised.

P. B. Whitehouse

Plate 209: The nameboard on Old Hill Station is genuine GWR, with cast-iron letters painted white and screwed on to a wooden background. The board was supported by standard cast-iron columns.

P. B. Whitehouse

Plate 210 (top left): Old Hill Station, just after nationalization, with 0-6-0 pannier tank No. 7435 alongside the Halesowen branch platform. On the right a Birmingham to Dudley diesel-mechanical railcar can be seen.

P. B. Whitehouse

Plate 211 (bottom left): The steeply-graded line from Old Hill to Halesowen, where it made a head on junction with the Midland Railway, opened in 1883, although the Midland section to Northfield (Halesowen Junction) did not take traffic until 1905. The branch's primary use was for freight, and public passenger services ceased in 1927 when competition from the roads began to take place. Morning and evening workmen's trains continued to run to Longbridge, for the Austin Works, until the 1960s. No. 7435 stands in the Old Hill branch platform, in the autumn of 1947, with the empty stock for Hockley. This class had just replaced the open cab 1813 class panniers.

P. B. Whitehouse

Plate 212: A very rare Halesowen Railway enamel notice. Although in poor condition, it would be almost priceless to a collector. It was in position on Hunnington Station.

P. B. Whitehouse

Plate 213: Halesowen Station in later years. The platforms were still in use for the workmen's morning and evening services.

P. B. Whitehouse

Plate 214: Out of the GWR era, but in early BR days, this is the only known photograph of one of these trains at Halesowen Station. The empty stock for a Longbridge to Old Hill workmen's train worked through to Longbridge double-headed by 57XX class 0-6-0 pannier tanks. This was in the later days of the service after Dowery Dell Viaduct, an exceedingly splendid structure, was passed for heavier axle loadings. Certainly, until the 1950s, the weight restrictions were strictly enforced with outside-framed ex-MR Kirtley 0-6-0s, later Class 2F 0-6-0s, working the freights and only the lighter weight pannier tanks, later the 74XX class, carrying out passenger work.

John Edgington

Plate 215: A Longbridge to Old Hill workmen's train approaches Old Hill Station behind 74XX class 0-6-0 pannier tank, No.7435.

P. B. Whitehouse

Great Western into Western

Plate 216:   Hereford Station in the summer of 1948, the first year of nationalization. In the platform is a north to west express from Shrewsbury, headed by No. 5020 *Trematon Castle,* still in GWR livery with the number on the front buffer beam and the roundel on the tender side. Note the second coach with doors to each compartment, which was standard practice before the introduction, in the 1930s, of wide window stock.

P. B. Whitehouse

Plate 217:   No. 5014 *Goodrich Castle* takes an early afternoon London express through the main line 'up' platform at Knowle and Dorridge Station on 26th August 1951. The engine carries an 81A (Old Oak Common) shed plate and a new cast-iron smokebox numberplate, but it is so dirty that the tender insignia is hidden. The leading vehicle appears to be one of the long 'Dreadnought' coaches (70ft.) of the 1904-7 period.

C. F. H. Oldham

Plate 218: One of the last of Churchward's 4-6-0 'Stars' to remain in service, No. 4056 *Princess Margaret* is seen at Snow Hill prior to setting out for Swindon Works with a Stephenson Locomotive Society special. The date is 9th September 1956 and the route is an unusual one, via Stourbridge Junction, Worcester, Hereford and Severn Tunnel Junction. Note Snow Hill North (electrically operated) signal box on stilts on the left-hand side of the photograph.

Eric Oldham